School Libraries
Head for the Edge

School Libraries Head for the Edge

Rants, Recommendations, and Reflections

Doug Johnson

A LINWORTH PUBLISHING BOOK

LIBRARIES UNLIMITED
An Imprint of ABC-CLIO, LLC

A B C ⬥ C L I O

Santa Barbara, California • Denver, Colorado • Oxford, England

Library of Congress Cataloging-in-Publication Data

Johnson, Doug, 1952–
    School libraries head for the edge : rants, recommendations, and reflections / Doug Johnson.
        p. cm.
    "A Linworth Publishing Book."
    Includes bibliographical references.
    ISBN-13: 978-1-58683-392-3 (pbk.)
    ISBN-10: 1-58683-392-8 (pbk.)
    1. School libraries—United States.   2. Instructional materials centers—United States.   3. School
librarians—Effect of technological innovations on—United States.   4. Instructional materials
personnel—Effect of technological innovations on—United States.   5. Media programs
(Education)—United States.   I. Title.
    Z675.S3J642   2009
    027.80973—dc22   2009022053

14   13   12   11   10   1   2   3   4   5

This book is also available on the World Wide Web as an eBook.
Visit www.abc-clio.com for details.

ABC-CLIO, LLC
130 Cremona Drive, P.O. Box 1911
Santa Barbara, California 93116-1911

This book is printed on acid-free paper ∞
Manufactured in the United States of America

To everyone who ever said "thank you" to me
for something I've written.
And of course to the LWW.

Table of Contents

Introduction: 800 Words

A conclusion is the place where you got tired of thinking.

—Harold Fricklestein

It all started with a rant.

In 1993 I was in my second year as a district library supervisor, and I was getting lots of pushback from the building librarians I had inherited. I was determined to make them technology-integration specialists, and they seemed just as determined to remain print-only librarians. After one particularly frustrating day, I turned on my computer, opened my e-mail, and just let rip about the reactionary, troglodytic, myopic, nature of school librarians, concluding that they had better damn well wake up and smell the coffee or they would all be replaced with technologists and not to let the door hit 'm where the good lord split 'm on the way out. And off the rant went to the then new international e-mail list, LM_NET.

Let me put it this way—I got some reaction. I knew librarians had good vocabularies, but even *I* learned some new words. I believe after that diatribe other LM_NETters opened my e-mails simply wondering what idiotic thing I might say next. In LM_NET I found my voice. And I convinced Marlene Woo-Lun and Carol Simpson at Linworth Publishing to put my little rants in their magazines.

"Head for the Edge" first appeared in Linworth's *Technology Connection* magazine, a predecessor to *Library Media Connection,* in February of 1995. The title of the first column was "Making Change Work for You." It was about 800 words, one page long. I've written about 80,000 more words for the column in the following 14 years.

These columns have been written, I'll admit, for a rather selfish reason. It is through writing that I reflect, distill, organize, and understand what is happening in my professional life. Being a reflective practitioner, the experts say, is a good thing. You could call these columns my "pre-blog blog."

Readers of this column have been generous with comments, criticisms, and praise. It's the rare conference I attend or week of e-mail that goes by that someone doesn't and say, "When reading *Library Media Connection,* I always turn to the last page first." Since I do exactly that with a number of magazines, I find it high praise indeed. Compliments are a strange combination of both ego gratification and satisfaction in knowing one has helped another person. Thanks to all who have offered them.

A few observations about writing this column. This part is not required reading.

1. It has always been a delight to work with editor Carol Simpson for most of the years I have been writing. She's a wonderful editor, a respected professional librarian, and an all-round class act. For all the stress I may have caused in the past 14 years, I apologize. In 2008, the esteemed Gail Dickinson took the editorial reins. So far, so good, but I am keeping a close eye on her. For those of you with an article in you that needs to escape to the larger professional community, you could do worse than sending it to Gail.

2. One of my guilty pleasures is re-reading my old columns. I've heard authors say that they cannot stand to read their older works because what they are currently working on is so much better. Other than wincing at an overuse of exclamation points, I still get tickled reading my own stuff. My wife thinks it's sick, but I can't help it. It's a delight when you recognize that what you wrote years ago still holds up pretty well.

3. I am struck by the lack of humor in most professional writing. Too many writers feel that in order to be taken seriously, they must always *be* serious. This is a mistake. We too often forget that in order to connect with another person intellectually, you have to connect emotionally as well.

4. The profession needs more writers who are willing to tackle our sacred cows. The best writing I've done is that which has kicked up the most dust. I'd like to see more writing on effective techniques for keeping one's job, ways to take ownership of the information literacy curriculum, passive resistance to state and federal mandates that are not in kids' best interest, and ways for making collaboration systemic and effective. My dad used to say that opinions are like, well, a certain anatomical feature—everyone has one. We need more people sharing those opinions. We're doing practice-based research every day we do our jobs. More people to need to share their knowledge.

5. Most of my columns are about opportunities embedded in the problems we face. We need to start looking for opportunities rather than simply complaining when something new comes on the educational scene. I certainly have my doubts about many of the educational

"silver bullets du jour." But I have also felt unprofessional knowing that I too have been a willing keeper of the dirty little secret that our schools continue to graduate students who are unprepared for life. Even a plan with flaws is at least an attempt to remedy the problems. We should stop complaining, and start determining what our roles should be in this era of educational accountability.

6. The librarian will always be the sole determining factor of quality of the library program. I've yet to see a great program run by a mediocre professional or a good professional that could not make significant improvements under the worst conditions. We are impatient, we hold ourselves to incredibly high standards, and we dream big. Those aren't bad things, but we also need to remember that our greatest accomplishments are when we improve, even a little, the life of an individual student. Providing that one book that was "just right," that one piece of elusive information, or that one life-long skill may have longer lasting ramifications than all the formal lessons we've taught or planned or taught. Change is made one person at a time. Make it a goal to help at least one person each day. Over the course of a career, you'll have made more of a difference than you'll ever know.

7. And finally, I will once again beat that same old drum—either we take responsibility for the technology in our lives and schools and master it and use it and be seen as the experts by others or we will be replaced by professionals who will.

I believe that the school library field has a bright and fascinating future. Remember, the one thing your library has that the Internet never will is YOU!

You will find *most* my columns here—the good, the bad, and the ugly—only slightly revised. Much like the author himself, they seem to be aging quite gracefully. The ones not included here are mostly the ones that have gone on to lead other lives as longer magazine articles or parts of my other books. They are printed in chronological order within general topic categories. I have deleted or updated some references and excluded URLs. Just google the title, for Pete's sake.

I hope you have as much fun reading or re-reading them as I had writing them.

All the best,
Doug

CHAPTER 1

On Libraries and Education in Transition

Making Change Work for You

February 1995

The Chinese have a wonderful curse: "May you live in interesting times." In education we are living in interesting times, indeed.

Downsizing, restructuring, role redefinition, site-based management, empowerment, technology, consolidation, co-location, and total quality management (TQM) seem to be the current educational buzzwords of choice. The number of school librarians in our region has shrunk, while the amount of work asked of those who remain has grown. As education changes because of the information explosion, everyone's role in it will change—including yours and mine. Now I happen to be rather fond of getting a paycheck, but I also know everyone's position is vulnerable to cuts.

Surviving Corporate Transition is a pretty awful title for a pretty good book (Bridges 1991). While William Bridge's audience and examples are from the business world, much of the theory he extols works just fine in schools. Bridges offers three valuable suggestions for keeping one's job.

Head for the edge. "The people who work along the interface between the organization and its external environment are the sources of all the information that is needed to survive in this rapidly changing world."

Are you, as your building's information expert, capitalizing on this important task? Do you read, filter, and direct information to your patrons who not only use it, but become dependent upon it? As information moves from print to digital format, are you the "interface" to the Internet, to online card catalogs and databases, and all forms of digital information?

Are you the school's emissary to other organizations in the community that also provide services to your users? Do you facilitate use of other libraries in the community? Can you tap into the information services and professionals of local post-secondary institutions, government agencies, business, and health care organizations?

This advice—"head for the edge"—is so apt for our profession that I've chosen it as the title for this column. By going to the edge and peering over, I hope we'll find some new ways to look at old ideas, some familiar ways to look new ideas, and begin to wonder and plan for what might be store for our profession.

Forget jobs and look for work that needs doing. "Security in turbulent times comes from doing something important for the organization, not from filling a long-standing position."

The most successful librarians I know listen to teachers' and principals' problems. Most educators aren't shy about sharing them. What in your building is important and may not be getting done? Developing interdisciplinary units? Providing staff development in technology? Caring for and circulating equipment? Serving on the site-based council? Chairing the parent-teacher association? Publishing the building newsletter? Advising student council? Managing computer networks and user accounts?

I've always had an affinity for jobs no one else wanted. Especially those that my boss liked to pass off. I always hoped that if my job and someone else's job were both on the line, my supervisor's reasoning might go thus: "If I fire Johnson, I'll have to find someone else to do all those nasty jobs he's taken on. Otherwise, I might have to do them myself. Hmmm, let's see who else I might axe instead . . ."

I would not be too narrow in my definition of a professional task either. It might be better to perform vital clerical or technical work, than an unnecessary "professional" duty.

Diversify your efforts into several areas of activity. "Like diversified investors, people with composite careers can balance a loss in one area with a gain in another. Consequently, they are not subject to the total disasters faced by people who have all their bets on one square."

Some librarians I know are removing their subject area teaching endorsement from their licenses. Now if you feel that if you can't have a job as a librarian, you'd rather not have a job in education at all, that's the thing to do. But unless you have a real good feeling about that last lottery ticket you bought, be aware that the employment outlook in the "real world" is even worse than it is in education. I know. I knew somebody who worked in business once.

The smart thing for those of us who still need to work to do is to *add* areas of endorsement. Coaching, English as a second language, middle school, administration, and reading certification all make one a "value-added" employee. In the same vein, a list of successfully completed projects, grants, or workshops show administrators that you are versatile, and will help you develop a "can do" reputation. If your history job is reduced or eliminated, there is a better chance of the school finding another position for you.

"Making Change Work For You" is the chapter from which these nuggets of wisdom were lifted, and the title captures the spirit of true proactivity. Remember also another saying—that the Chinese word for crisis is made of two separate characters: one meaning danger, the other meaning opportunity!

The Sound of the Other Shoe Dropping

March 1995

Where can I find answers to these reference questions while not leaving my desk?

- What is the atomic weight of boron or the size of the Andromeda galaxy?
- Are there any bookstores in Albuquerque, New Mexico, that carry a book by Krol on computing?
- Last year the federal Department of Education proposed a new technology policy. Where can I find the text of this policy?
- What nights will the Denver Nuggets be playing home basketball games this season?
- What was the total amount of sales in liquor stores in the United States in September of this year? Was it more than last year?
- What's been written on the development of hiking trails for the handicapped?
- I've heard Clairol offers college scholarships. How do I qualify?
- Where can I get the monthly Consumer Price Index for the last decade as a computer file that can be imported into a spreadsheet?

Well, on the Internet, of course. Should this information source be of interest to librarians? It is more than interesting—it's critical to the survival of our profession.

Your answer to one question will tell if you'll be one of the survivors in the great print information to digital information shift: Why are you in the profession?

At the turn of the century, this country had lots of blacksmiths. Some stayed employed and some didn't. Why? If you asked the soon-to-be-unemployed blacksmiths why they were in the business, they'd have said, "Because I like horses." If you asked the other blacksmiths, those who stayed viable in their changing environment, the same question, they probably said, "Because I like helping people get from place to place."

When the first horseless carriage came along, those with the transportation mission fixed wheels, banged out fenders, and even tinkered under the hood. They remained transportation specialists.

Ask yourself the same question: Why am I in the library profession? "Because I like books" is the wrong answer. I hope you said, "Because I like helping people find, use, and communicate the things they need to know."

As computers fill our schools, you're probably helping kids with search strategies, banging out reports with desktop publishers, completing Webquests and even investigating the invisible Web. You've remained an information specialist.

Unfortunately, we as a profession have a history of dropping the ball when it comes to making new technologies our own. In how many schools is the audiovisual department still separate from library? In how many schools is the librarian not seen as a computer expert, even though we all know that a tremendous amount of information is available to patrons in electronic formats? In how many schools are keyboarding, word processing, database and spreadsheet use, and computer-assisted drawing no part of the information literacy curriculum, even though two-thirds of our mission is teach students to process and communicate information?

How many of us are seen as teacher prep time babysitters, rather than critical components of the total educational process, and are thus expendable in tight economic times?

Our profession currently has a tremendous opportunity to become relevant information experts—*if* we have the willingness and determination to learn something challenging. And keep learning.

I once read an Internet signature that taunted, "Libraries are for people who can't afford modems." Ouch. But if a critical mass of librarians doesn't become the on-line information specialists for teachers, students, and administrators, the next sound we hear won't be that of a ball being dropped, but the sound of the other shoe.

New Resources, New Selection Skills

April 1996

Twice this year I have been asked to give talks on "The Best of the Internet for Kids." After only very short consideration, I decided that this was an extremely daunting task. With the millions of Web sites alone available, any short list that could be shared would have to be eclectic indeed, and shortly out of date. I'd compare giving such a talks as being asked to booktalk a library.

It is certainly possible to share some exemplary sites for young people, whether those sites have been created specifically for them or are adult sites that are of use and interest. It's also worthwhile to list a few "jump sites" to child- or school-oriented materials on the Internet. I suspect we all have our favorites. And given a lab for hands-on training, time could not be better spent than finding, using, and comparing search engines and strategies.

I submit, however, that in our role, we should be helping teachers and students develop usable evaluative standards for Internet resources instead of just pointing out some good ones. Haven't we always prided ourselves on teaching folks how to fish rather than simply providing that walleye?

Below are a few standards for evaluating good Web sites I share when asked to give those "Best of the Internet" talks. This list is by no means exclusive, and you'll quickly note that many of the standards apply to all information resources.

Does the source have some subject authority? Is there actual content at the site? The author should clearly state his credentials, and if the information is critical, the credentials need to be verified. There are no editors on the Internet to help filter out the sludge.

Can the source be judged impartial? If this source is written or sponsored by a commercial sponsor, are we alert to bias? Do we apply the same standards to commercially sponsored Internet resources as we do to other commercially produced educational products? Check out the

"Guidelines for Evaluating SOCAP & IOCU Materials" written by the Consumers Union (1998).

Is the information timely? Does the page include the date of its last revision? It's surprising how many Internet files are birthed and then abandoned.

Is the site age-appropriate for content and vocabulary? This one is as tricky for Web pages as it is for print materials. There are sites that have been created just for children, but are little more than blatant product endorsements I would not select, while NASA and the Center for Disease Control have resources published for an adult audience that can provide excellent information for elementary students.

Is the site well organized? Are there links back to the home page from lower level pages? Does the homepage serve as an accurate table of contents to the rest of the site? Non-linear organizational structures still need a logical arrangement. Lengthy menus need sub-menus, pages need to be clearly categorized, and it's always nice when the topic of the page bears a resemblance to the category under which it was found. Pages themselves should be organized. Considerate Web page writers put links back to the site's homepage on every page at a site.

Are the links on the page to other sites relevant to the subject? Are the pages regularly checked to see if the links are still valid? Again, check for revision dates.

Does the site preserve bandwidth by using graphics to convey information and not just for visual appeal? Have thumbnail graphics that link users to large picture files been provided for those of us with less than stellar connections to the Internet? Are large amounts of textual information divided into smaller pages for faster downloading?

Developing "selection" standards for Internet sites should be a natural for our profession. We need to be asking ourselves:

- What is it that makes a search engine useful?
- How can I quickly tell if a newsgroup or blogger is worth following?
- What criteria can I use if asked to recommend a listserv?
- Are there identifiable qualities of a good e-mail message?

And more importantly, we should be teaching our students to ask such questions.

The 21st-Century Teacher

May 1999

It's been about two years now since I came up behind two fifth grade boys as they sat giggling at an Internet terminal in one of our school libraries. "Oh, oh," I suspiciously thought, "What are they into that they shouldn't be?"

As it turns out, they were in one of the Center for Disease Control's computers down in Atlanta looking up information about the Ebola virus. Pretty cool for 10-year-olds, I thought, and left it at that. But the more I considered the incident, the more remarkable its implications became. There are some very real, very sudden changes happening to teachers and teaching right now. And the availability of the Internet is almost single-handedly bringing those changes about. And we who provide staff development for our teaching partners need to be aware of these changes.

It's taken the presence of the Internet to highlight what dramatic impact geography has had on education. The teachers, the resources, and the experiences to which most of us B.C. (Before Computing) students had access were those within our communities. We learned what our teachers knew. We had access only to the teachers within our own school. We learned the core values of only our community since those values were the only ones to which we had much exposure. What might be some of the implications of students having access to a virtual world that is beginning to erase those geographic limits?

What is being taught will change. How will the dynamics of the classroom change when the boys return armed with their new information about the Ebola virus?

Most apparently, student interest, probably peaked by newspaper articles, television programs, or local issues, rather than a set curriculum has begun to drive learning. Teachers in the 21st century will need to know how to take areas of high student interest, often self-selected, and use them to teach the important concepts for their grade or content area. Using problems related to the Ebola virus, for example, the teacher will still be teaching writing, reading, mathematics, health and safety, science, history, and civics. But the struggle for student relevance and interest is half-won. The class is already "about" a topic that students have judged to be important.

The less obvious change is in the instructional role of the classroom teacher. The students, not the teacher nor textbook, have suddenly become the content experts on the Ebola virus. And consequently, teachers need to redefine their roles to stay relevant to the learning process. Now instead of dispensing facts and opinions about the disease, the teacher will need to know how to start asking questions like:

- Where and how did you find your information?
- How do you know if that is a reliable source?
- How can you use the information you found to make a difference in your life or in your community?
- How can you help others understand this information?

It's easy to see that great 21st-century teaching will be more important than it has ever been in the past as educators move from being knowledge builders rather than knowledge dispensers. Great teachers, unlike books or videos, will be truly interactive.

Who is doing the teaching will change. Right now, if I want to learn to design a Web page I can take any number of online classes, often taught by national experts. I am no longer tied to the local community education classes, technical school classes, or university classes whose teachers may or may not be effective. Increasingly all students will have an option to sitting through classes with poor, disinterested teachers or with teachers whose teaching style simply doesn't suit their own learning styles.

Online courses are here and growing in number. As more states begin to describe graduation requirements in terms of what students should know and be able to do, rather than how much time they need to be in a desk, the feasibility of alternatives to physical classrooms and traditional teaching begins to grow.

Excellence in teaching and course design will be essential when it is no more difficult to take a class offered in a school across the country than it is to take one next door. As Elliott Masie of the Masie Center reminds us:

> There is no social pressure to "stay," when learning online. If you attend an instructor-led class and are bored or not pleased with the content, you will probably stick it out, at least until lunch or the end of the day. We have been conditioned to stay and tolerate less than optimal classes. However,

our social conditioning when online is the exact opposite. We are always one click away from departure.

Mediocrity won't last long where there are choices. For great teachers, the golden age of education is here. For poor teachers—"Be afraid. Be very afraid."

The way that "values" instruction will change. Let's look at those questions that the 21st-century teacher will need to be at asking again:

- Where and how did you find your information?
- How do you know if that is a reliable source?
- How can you use the information you found to make a difference in your life or in your community?
- How can you help others understand this information?

For none of these questions is there a simple, right-or-wrong response. Each requires higher-level thinking and the ability to articulate and defend individual values. As individuals we will need to ask and answer for ourselves, for example, how much credibility governments (Center for Disease Control), the media (the popular book *Hot Zone* and *Newsweek*), business (insurance companies and HMOs), and individuals (personal Web pages and talk show callers) each have. Teachers themselves will need to be comfortable with the choices they have made for themselves in order to guide their students.

While it's pretty difficult to be "for" a communicable disease, other topics that student will be faced with are more controversial. The role of the United States in world affairs, the continuation of affirmative action policies, the role of the government in health care and education, and freedom of expression are all important topics, topics that should be of relevance to our students. And our wired children will be hearing a cacophony of voices about these issues. The teacher's role increasingly will be one that helps students make sense of the noise and make good choices based on that sense.

School librarians, if you think your job has changed over the past few years, you ain't seen nothing until teachers start to change. Some are already there. Some will make the transition smoothly and joyfully. Some will gracefully take early retirement or find another line of work. It's the rest who will make our lives interesting. All teachers will be looking to us as models, as co-teachers, and as suppliers of materials, tools, skills, and support. Let's be there for them.

What Happened to the Good Old Days of Education?

November 2001

I'm sure this never happens where you live, but public education here in Minnesota gets criticized on a regular basis. And I just don't understand it.

In my 25 years as a teacher, school librarian, and administrator in the K–12 schools, I have never worked with better teachers in finer facilities with more resources—all combining to produce better educated graduates. Yet our governor has called schools the "black hole" of state spending. Newspaper letter writers question why the bare-bones schools of one teacher, 30 students, a pencil sharpener, and the 3r's curriculum of their youth (and look how good *I* turned out) aren't sufficient today.

This chart from the book *Teaching the New Basic Skills* may help explain why it often seems the better schools get, the more harsh the criticism (Murnane 1997). Each block represents the percent of the kinds of jobs available to students leaving high school in various years. Back in the days of Wally and the Beav, 60 percent of kids leaving school went to work in non-skilled jobs. If you followed directions well, showed up for work regularly, had a high tolerance for boredom and a strong back, there was a job for you on the factory floor or on the farm. The basic skills were enough, and many folks left school before

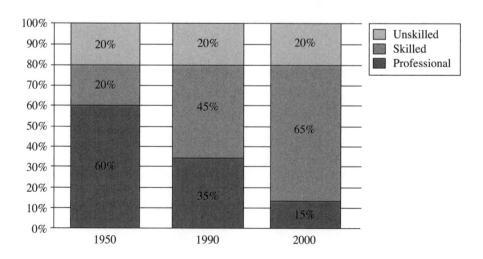

even having mastered readin' and writin' and were still able to support a family with the kinds of jobs available to them.

Fast-forward 50 years. With factories being automated and farm labor supplanted by applied science, only 15 percent of jobs now available can be considered "unskilled." 85 percent of today's students need the same skills and education that only about 40 percent needed in the "good old days." There is no longer a place in the workforce for those very quiet or very loud kids we knew from our own days as students who just slipped through by virtue of seat time without ever really learning to read or write, let alone think critically, communicate successfully, be self-motivated, develop organizational skills, and creatively solve problems. Today's employers actually need well-educated workers for almost every job they offer.

Of course the children that come to school are so much easier to teach today than in the 1950s. *Not!* In our small-town, middle-class enclave right here in the Midwest:

- The number of students coming from financially needy families has grown 35 percent in the past 15 years.

- Our special education student population has increased 76 percent in the past 15 years.

- Our English as a second language student population has increased 122 percent over just the past few years.

And of course everyone who has taught in the schools for any length of time knows that we see more and more children who come from single-parent families; have serious drug problems; or are just plain addicted to televisions or video games. Where is the child who lives in the house with the white picket fence next door to Ozzie and Harriet who heads to school each morning with her lunch lovingly packed by Mom after having been tutored by Dad the evening before? The students we teach are wonderful—the best kids ever. But they are certainly no easier to teach and maybe more difficult to reach than those of previous generations.

The problem is not that our schools are not getting better; they are simply not getting better fast enough.

What does this mean to us as librarians and technology directors? A few things:

- The chart points out to me as an educator that much of our effort must be to teach those kids who in the 1950s did not need to be taught. As we design our research projects and reading programs, we must increase our efforts on the kids who may have just been passed on along in the Beaver's classroom. They too need to be problem-solvers and life-long learners or there won't much of a job out there for them.

- We need to find new ways to motivate and challenge learners who may not come from a culture in which education may not be viewed as important. We must learn to connect with not just the mind but also the heart of each student who comes to us.

- As a profession we cannot apologize for the costs of the additional resources we need to educate all children, not just those few going on to college.

Each and every one of us needs to loudly voice our professional opinion on the need for better libraries, highly qualified and remunerated educators, effective technologies, and good facilities. It is unprofessional for us to do any less.

The "M" Word

January 2003

We should all be obliged to appear before a board every five years and justify our existence . . . on pain of liquidation.

—George Bernard Shaw

If the current economic trends continue, I expect this spring to be preparing for yet another storm of budget cuts swirling around my district. This is no isolated shower. This weather front runs across the nation. As the clouds gather, listen carefully, and throughout the maelstrom you'll hear it: the M-word in loud and rueful voices.

"What we really need our legislature to do is *mandate* that every school have a library program!"

Ah, those magic mandates. Let's require by law that every student in our state have access to a good school library collection and librarian. The research says it's a good thing for a whole raft of reasons. Isn't there a way we can simply circumvent, with a good law or two, these local troglodytes who refuse to be enlightened about school libraries?

To be honest, I am not terribly excited about mandated anything. We all agree that strong school library programs are in the best interest of students, teachers, and communities. It's how to achieve this effectively that I worry about.

As I hear about cuts in library positions being made across the country, this is what I would be asking of those whose jobs are in jeopardy: "What tasks are you doing that are so important that it will be a huge problem for administrators to find others to do them?"

My state of Minnesota has not had mandates for school library programs for many years. When we did have "The Rule," it was so routinely ignored that it was nearly meaningless. That is why, like it or not:

- Our district's elementary librarians teach and assess a required part of the state standards and give grades to all students on information literacy, technology skills, life-long reading behaviors, and appropriate use.
- Our district's elementary librarians cover prep time.
- Our district's librarians are the webmasters for their buildings.
- Our district's librarians have network administration duties.
- Our district's librarians are in charge of *Accelerated Reader* in the buildings that use it.
- Our district's librarians do staff development in technology.
- Our district's librarians serve on building site teams.
- Our district's librarians go to parent-teacher organization meetings.
- Our district's librarians serve on curriculum committees.
- Our district's librarians meet each year with their building principals to make sure they know their buildings' goals and work with the building leadership to make sure the library's goals and budget directly support the building goals.

If they fire our district's librarians, I will at least have the satisfaction of knowing the principals will suffer as well because they will need to find others to do these critical tasks.

It is also why, like it or not, every librarian takes *personal* responsibility for making sure that as many people as possible (especially those in our community) know about the research that ties library and technology programs to improved academic performance and what our own school's programs are doing to improve student learning.

I don't think I am overly idealistic in my mandate-free approach to keeping library positions. Two years ago, our district formed a "choice" elementary school of about 90 students. It's a model for many new schools we are seeing here in Minnesota—very small, project-based, hugely individualized, and teacher-governed. The first year the leadership team chose to staff a .1 librarian position. The next year they decided they did not need the position. When they struggled that year with many tasks that that person had done the prior year, they reinstated a .25 librarian position the following year.

When one works without the mandate net, one tends to pay more attention to the needs of those one serves and perhaps a little less attention to theoretical "best practices." Best practices are those that keep school libraries vital and indispensable by providing the services that are seen as important by the entire institution. We need to acknowledge that other people in education also have valid perspectives about what is in the best interest of the children we all serve. I know it is exceedingly hard to admit, but we school librarians may not always have all the answers. (However, we do have them a frighteningly high percentage of the time.)

We also need to recognize that many, many people resent mandates and the people who are in schools as a result of them. Mandates don't insure quality, only quantity. Mandates can give the person mandated a false sense of security and an excuse for not providing indispensable services. Mandates can protect the less competent in our profession whose image then reflects on the rest of us. In an image-challenged profession, who needs that? Even great programs can be endangered by mandates if the need for good communications is not seen as critical and they slip into invisibility.

There are lots of things I'd love to mandate. But expending huge amounts of energy and political capital in trying to get them is akin to spitting in the wind. State library organizations should look carefully at national and state trends in education. Fewer and fewer mandates and other requirements are coming to schools from all levels of government. All types of requirements are being replaced by accountability reporting. In other words, states and the feds are saying—"Here is what you have to do and how to prove it. We don't care how you choose to get it done."

Our profession needs to recognize this trend and prepare our members to meet the challenges this political wind is blowing in by providing tools, techniques, and training to empower the building-level librarian.

Help is available. Check out the advocacy tools provided by the American Association of School Libraries (AASL).

As the Arab proverb reminds us, "It's easier to steer the camel in the direction it is already running."

Exposing Shameful Little Secrets

January 2004

Brian was a school-wide secret we all guiltily shared: a senior who would graduate but could not read.

In 1976, I started my career in education as the world's worst high school English teacher. In every class, I soon discovered a significant number of "Brians" who could not comprehend even the least challenging materials.

Teaching a full-time load, sponsoring multiple extracurricular activities; and moonlighting at a gas station left me little time to deal with Brian, so he and I struck the same unspoken deal he'd made with his other teachers: "I'll behave in your class; you'll pass me with a D."

I feel guilty to this day that I kept the secret that doomed Brian to a life of illiteracy.

Fast forward to 1996. Foreshadowing the No Child Left Behind Act (NCLB), Minnesota instituted an eighth-grade reading test that students needed to pass to graduate from high school. Suddenly the Brians were outed. My school could no longer hide those students who could not demonstrate a minimum level of reading proficiency. The state released numbers comparing how many Brians we had compared to other schools. As a result, something unprecedented happened. The district reached deep into its pockets and found the spare change necessary to provide remedial instruction for the Brians. By the time that first group of eighth graders graduated, all but one read well enough to at least pass the test.

The professional literature is filled with condemnations of the No Child Left Behind law. But are educators so busy criticizing the means that they've forgotten the goal of the program: that schools must address the learning needs of every student?

NCLB requires districts to disaggregate student test scores by ethnic and other subgroups. In doing so, our high performing school found that its LEP (limited English proficiency) students lagged in achievement compared to other LEP students in the state. Guess what? The district is actively studying the problem, and my crystal ball says it will find the where-with-all needed to improve the LEP program very quickly.

Rather than dwelling on ulterior political motives, educators—especially librarians—should work to meet the spirit of the legislation by using it as a springboard for improving instruction for struggling students. Librarians can help by:

Designing reading programs and providing materials especially for the groups causing a school to be identified as not making AYP (Adequate Yearly Progress). Smart schools are figuring out that just increasing standard reading instruction does not work and are looking for other strategies, including having children extensively read materials of high interest. Our library programs are critical partners in such programs.

Modifying and improving research assignments for at risk students. Ruby Payne makes a compelling argument in her book *A Framework for Understanding Poverty* (2003) that students living in poverty need assignments that are relevant, applicable to everyday life, and personal. Our information literacy projects should be modified to help meet the needs of those kids.

Helping educate the public about alternative ways of assessing student performance. One scary aspect of NCLB is its overreliance on standardized tests as a measurement of student performance. The general public believes such tests are reliable, objective, and understandable despite the fact they measure only a few basic skills and penalize students who are poor test-takers. Assessment tools that assess higher-level thinking skills and the application of skills are also necessary. As librarians, we need to keep using and promoting authentic assessment tools and educating parents about their usefulness.

Gaining awareness of the NCLB requirements and lobbying for change. As school leaders, librarians should be helping educate the public about all dimensions of effective schools and the problems in the NCLB law. Can a school be "good" if NCLB deems it not meeting "adequate yearly progress"? Certainly in many ways. Do school reforms that truly insure that "no child is left behind" cost money? Most likely. Could public education be weakened instead of strengthened as a result of NCLB? Perhaps. We need to get and stay informed and find venues to express our concerns to the public and our legislators.

We may never meet the ambitious NCLB literacy goal of 100 percent by 2013. But as we learned in Minnesota with our reading test, it may get us closer to that goal. It is in our professional and students' best interests if we look upon NCLB as a challenge and an impetus for change—not simply an injustice to rail against.

None of us should have to keep a secret like Brian.

Schools Are More than the Sum of Their Scores

March 2004

In the previous column, I suggested that the No Child Left Behind Act might indeed help keep some students from failing to become literate. At its heart, NCLB's goal of making sure all students are well educated is right on target. The downside, of course, is the act's over-reliance on test scores as the measurement of student achievement. It simply ignores many of the other qualities that are more difficult to measure that make a school, well, a school.

To help parents here in Minnesota determine if their local schools are any good, our Department of Education has followed the lead of other states and created a report card for each school with a "star" rating system of one to five. These stars are based on good, hard, no nonsense data, harumpff. Right now, this simplistic system relies on state test scores—period.

I suspect our DOE got the idea from reading movie reviews. The number of thumbs or bags of popcorn gives a potential moviegoer a quick indication if he should even read the review, let alone see the movie. Rating schools, however, is tad more serious. It's one thing to blow a couple hours and a few dollars on a crummy film. It's quite another to entrust your child to a truly bad school.

I hope our parents look at the state report cards (they do tell *something*), but continue looking beyond them as well. As a parent, I'd also rate my schools based on these "stars":

Star One: School climate. It's funny how a person can sense the safety, friendliness, and sense of caring within minutes of walking into a school. Little things like cleanliness, displays of student work, open doors to classrooms, laughter, respectful talk, presence of volunteers, and genuine smiles from both adults and kids are the barometers of school climate. If a school doesn't earn this star, a parent doesn't need to bother looking at the other criteria. Get your kids out quickly. (How can our library and technology programs contribute to our building's climate?)

Star Two: Libraries and technology. The quality of the library is the clearest sign of how much a school values reading, teaching for independent thinking, and life-long learning. A trained school librarian and a welcoming environment with a well-used collection of current books, magazines and computers with Internet access tell a parent that the teachers and principal value more than the memorization of facts from a text book, that a diversity of ideas and opinions is important, and that reading is not just necessary, but pleasurable and important. (How can we help the public understand this?)

Star Three: Individual teacher quality. This is why total school rating systems aren't very helpful. Five-star teachers are found in one-star schools and one-star teachers are found in five-star schools. I always listened to what other parents said about the teachers my children might have, and insisted that my kids got the *teachers* with good reviews. (How can librarian and technology people help improve teacher skills?)

Star Four: Elective and extracurricular offerings. What happens in class is important. But so is what happens during the other 18 hours of the day. Elementary schools need to offer after-school clubs and activities that develop social skills and interests. Secondary schools must be rich with art, sports, technology education, music and community service choices that develop individual talents, leadership, and pride in accomplishment. (Are our libraries and computer resources used at times outside the school day?)

Star Five: Commitment to staff development. The amount of exciting scientifically based research on effective teaching practices and schools is overwhelming. Brain-based research, reflective practice, systematic examination of student work, strategies for working with disadvantaged students are some of the latest findings that can have a positive impact on how we can best teach children. But research doesn't do a lick of good if it never gets out of the universities or scholarly journals. Good schools give financial priority to teaching teachers how to improve their practice. (Are we spending our library budgets, time and efforts in offering staff development activities for teachers, not just on technology, but on current best practices in education?)

School reports are a part of ratcheting up competition among schools. Schools with high test scores wave them like a banner to attract parent-consumers. But schools' public relations efforts need to go beyond bragging about just stars that are test-based and need to include other quality criteria as well. Does your school use the quality of your library program as part of its marketing efforts?

I hope stars and state report cards put some schools on notice that improvement is necessary. But I also hope we can help parents look beyond the stars.

The Importance of Bricks

September 2006

> Our district is in the process of planning a new high school. The architects are here and are saying that "many new schools are being built without libraries," and that "students will each have their own individual gizmo and be able to access everything they need online." (sigh)
>
> —from LM_NET, April 2, 2006.

A bit of a professional storm was raised last spring when a Texas librarian sent the message that included the quote above. That Texas—always the educational trendsetter!

As schools look for ways to economize and as students increasingly have access to and a preference for online information sources, the old "Why do we need a library when we have the Internet?" question will be asked more often and more loudly.

While many out front librarians have responded to this digital threat by offering an increasing amount of digital content and digital services, might I suggest that we must refocus our attention on our bricks and mortar facilities and face-to-face services rather than on our virtual resources if libraries and the field of librarianship are to survive. As counterintuitive as it may sound, the very ubiquity of information requires this. What can our physical libraries do that the Internet cannot?

Libraries must be the technology place. The library should house the infrastructure technologies needed to insure that students, teachers and their electronic tools can connect to each other and the rest of the world, where data and video servers, patch panels, and routers are placed in a secure area. It is the logical place to house the technical staff, where one of the professional librarian's jobs will be to help them prioritize their tasks and possibly supervise. The production lab containing computers with massive processing power used to do high-end image and video processing and number crunching will be a part of tomorrow's library. Also needed will be spaces and resources for individual tutoring and group teaching of information and technology skills.

Libraries must be the collaborative space. Collaborative learning and the need for social interaction will require our libraries to be places of active learning. Studies of Net Genners tell us that even this wired group wants and needs places for face-to-face interaction—a role a library space can fill in ways the classroom cannot. And while most of a child's education will be increasingly individualized to meet specific learning goals and styles, interpersonal and collaborative skills will become ever more important. This means conference rooms, small lounge spaces, and tables where talking is not just allowed, but expected.

Libraries must be the performance/demonstration location. I personally hope that storytelling, puppetry, live debates and demonstrations will be part of every child's education. The library needs to be the space where all steps of the information process are practiced—including communication. Every library needs a presentation/storytelling area with multimedia equipment and seating for groups larger than a class.

Libraries must be the relaxation/meditation/caffeination station. The library will remain a physical learning space only if we begin creating facilities and environments where kids and teachers want to be. The library must have comfortable chairs, a pleasant ambiance, and a friendly, low-stress, safe, and forgiving atmosphere. It must contain flexible spaces that can be used by individuals, small groups, and whole classes. Think about why one goes to Barnes & Noble rather than simply shops on Amazon. And yes, libraries should have coffee shops or their age-appropriate equivalent.

Libraries must be the go-to the place for face-to-face. As librarians, we will need to compete for patrons and promote our space since we are no longer the only game in town for information. It will be our skills, especially our interpersonal skills, to which patrons will be drawn. The librarian needs to be a good reason to go to the library, rather than to avoid the library, if we are to survive.

We forget sometimes that society has given our K-12 schools three major charges:

- Teach young people academic and technical skills.
- Socialize future citizens.
- Contain and protect children while Mom and Pop are busy.

Each of these societal charges is increasing, not lessening—hence all-day kindergarten, latchkey programs, longer school days, and longer school years.

Schools themselves will be made of bricks and mortar for as long as they are expected to provide not just educational, but socialization and custodial services by the public. And a space called a "library" must be integral to future schools.

How to Destroy Any School Library Program

March 2008

From: "Screwdisk" <sdisk666@inferno.org>
To: "Wormwood" <wormie@terrafirma.edu>
Subject: How to destroy any school library program
Date: Thur March 6, 2008:10:19 -0500
X-Mailer: Microsoft Outlook 9.2
Importance: Scorching

My dearest Wormwood:

Once again it is my unpleasant duty to report that your job performance in the area of retarding human potential was unsatisfactory during the past year, earning you a paltry two brimstones out of ten. At *all* the schools in your area, young humans are graduating at higher rates, are displaying a distressing tendency to do more of their own thinking, and are actually seeming to enjoy reading, problem solving and even, Hades help us, learning. This cannot continue if we have an ice cube's chance in hell of keeping mankind ignorant, cruel, and brutal.

The single common denominator among your schools is that they all have great school library programs. Once again it seems you've been playing *Bejeweled* instead being attentive at our staff meetings and have missed suggestions for crippling the school library program.

The fiendishly glorious thing about library programs is that their strength depends upon but a single fragile soul—that of the school librarian. You get to her, the entire program goes up in flames. [Evil chuckle, evil chuckle.]

You must convince "madam" or "master" librarian to:

- Think of the library as *her* program where *she* sets all the rules, knows all the best practices, and owns all the materials.

- Invite children into the library, but when they actually get there, set rules and expectations that make them feel uncomfortable, even unwelcome.

- Place more emphasis on getting stuff back and keeping it in order than getting it out and into kids' hands.

- Consider the only productive behaviors in the library to be academic in nature. Let it be known that pursuits of self-interest are simply a waste of resources.

- Assume that kids who like getting information in ways other than reading are rather slow or lazy. Oh, and treat them that way. Let it be known that books are superior to technology in every way, under every circumstance.

- Spend a lot of time making sure the cataloging meets standards. Stay in the back office while doing so. Don't let people say "anal retentive" like it's a bad thing.

- Ban the copy/paste command. Make students work for their plagiarized term papers!

- Ban cell phones. Ban mp3 players. Ban personal laptops. Ban games.

- Block YouTube. Block blogs. Block chat. Block games. Block Google Images. Block joke sites. Set as many rules on computer use as possible. For first time misuse, take away computer privileges for a minimum of a year.

- Only select and booktalk items he likes to read. Make sure he ignores any nonfiction titles. Claim graphic novels are the devil's handiwork.

- Make sure her library goals in no way relate to building or district goals.

- Assume teachers who do not want to collaborate are bad teachers and treat them as such. Assume administrators who do not automatically value the library are dolts and treat them as such.

- Always advocate for what is in the best interest of the library—not the library user.

- Never accept a task that she considers beneath her professional dignity—teaching a class, hosting a study hall, monitoring a test, keeping a Web site up-to-date, or managing a network.
- Develop an adversarial relationship with as many people as possible. Key are the principal, the custodian, the secretary and especially the technology director.
- Learn to play good cop/bad cop with the library aide, with the librarian being the bad cop.
- Make sure she is very, very fussy about her job title.
- Consider everything a collaborative effort, and take no responsibility for that which could be directly attributed to or blamed on him.
- Develop a good relationship with parents—only after she finds out her job may be cut.
- Whine. At every opportunity.

Remember to invoke the pernicious imps of Fear, Powerlessness and Defensiveness at every opportunity. A confident librarian, one that both children and adults like and respect, is among the worst of Our enemies! If Earth is ever to truly become the devil's playground, nasty concepts like critical thinking, tolerance for a diversity of opinions, the ability to empathize with others, and intellectual freedom must be stamped out faster than prison-made license plates. With even the least diligence and effort on your part, libraries that support these heresies can be rendered ineffectual by the simple corruption of a single soul.

Fire up, Wormwood! Fire up! Get these librarians in your schools heading down the wrong path. And do make sure it is "down."

Insincerely,

Screwdisk

With apologies to C. S. Lewis, of course.

The Other Shoe Redux

November 2008

. . . we as a profession have a history of dropping the ball when it comes to making new technologies our own . . . In how many schools is the librarian not seen as a computer expert, even though we all know that a tremendous amount of information is available to patrons in electronic format? In how many schools are word processing, database and spreadsheet use, and computer-assisted drawing no part of the library skills curriculum, even though two-thirds of our mission is teaching students to process and communicate information?

—"Sound of the Other Shoe Dropping,"
Head for the Edge, March 1995

If we take an honest look at what we as librarians have done since technology has come into our buildings, as painful as it is to say, we have dropped the ball—big time. Why?

Sexism. OK, let's just start out with the one reason that will get me in the most trouble. Our profession is comprised of about 90+ percent women. Brilliant, dedicated, hardworking women, but women who are subject to the same sexism that pervades society as a whole. Ideas coming from the field of librarianship are not given attention and seriousness because the majority of its practitioners are women. Guys rule school administration, and as technology came into schools, its implementation was turned over to the guy math teacher, not the female librarian. In our district, 12 out of 17 of our principals are male; 11 out of 12 of our librarians are female. Who gets heard?

Our own profession has a gender-bias. When AASL closed its 2005 conference with "a panel of leading figures in the school library field," all five were men. What has the male/female ratio of keynote speakers at your library and tech conferences looked like over the last decade?

Is the subtext in education, been "don't you librarians worry your pretty little heads about technology -just leave it to us manly men?" Well, girls?

Schizophrenia. The school library field divides itself pretty cleanly and clearly between the children's/young adult lit people and the research skills/technology people. And to a large extent, the lit people are in control.

The Nov/Dec 2007 issue of AASL's *Knowledge Quest* is a telling example. I was very excited to learn that the theme was "Intellectual Freedom 101." But I was very disappointed in reading it to find that the majority of the issue was devoted to book challenges—not Internet censorship and filtering problems. What does this say about the librarian's role in technology integration when we still seem to be more concerned about a few cranks wanting to strike a couple fiction books from our shelves than we are about an entire generation of children losing access to a broad range of online information sources and tools? The teachers I talk to don't worry about kids getting access to *Harry Potter,* but to Wikipedia, YouTube, blogs and wikis.

Until our profession sees its primary instructional focus as teaching information and technology literacy skills, we will lack both credibility and voice in technology implementation efforts.

Strategy. If librarians had a coat of arms, collaboration would have to be one of the biggest symbols on it. Our profession has books, articles, standards, workshops, and probably t-shirts and coffee mugs all devoted to collaboration with teachers in designing and implementing good information literacy and technology experiences into the curriculum.

But the emphasis has always been one-to-one, never the kind of systematic, whole-school collaborative approach that Technology Learning Coordinators Justin Medved and Dennis Harter from the International School of Bangkok described to me in a personal e-mail as their school-based approach to technology integration:

> We had to create a shared understanding of what 21st century learning is and why it's important. We had to allow them [the teaching staff] to help frame the context in which this could work at ISB.

Do we need to ask ourselves if the library field has put the cart before the horse, working with individual teachers before there is a school-wide understanding of information and technology literacy in place? Should we have been "collaborating" with our curriculum committees, our leadership teams, assessment coordinators and our staff development committees instead—and first? Without whole school buy-in, we may have amazing successes with a few individual teachers, but not impact the entire learning community. Is it too late for us to re-strategize?

Every criticism I've made can be applied to my own district and its library/technology program. But if librarianship as a profession is to survive and thrive, we need to have some hard conversations about who we are, what we do, and how we do it.

I will end this with the same words I ended the March 1995 column:

> . . . if a critical mass of librarians don't become the online information specialists . . . , the next sound we hear won't be that of a ball being dropped, but the sound of the other shoe.

Reflection

> The future is already here—it is just unevenly distributed.
>
> —William Gibson

If the past 20 years in education could be summarized by a single word, that word is change. And if I weren't writing for professional publication, I'd probably state: "Change is a bitch." Thank goodness I have more sense than to say something that crude in public.

For many of us the pace of change is terrifying. New tools and techniques and ideas come at us with a blizzard like force. We actually experience Lewis Carroll's terrible line "Now, here, you see, it takes all the running you can do, to keep in the same place." He was describing today's schools. Indeed, today's world.

And yet some changes are coming far too slowly. Where is the 24/7 access to information devices for all kids; those individualized education plans for every student; and the engaging lessons that technology can provide? Why has educational technology's promise gone largely unmet? "Why is not all kids learning?" as W so eloquently stated.

Why have librarians not embraced their role as technology and change agent in their organizations? Why have too many libraries and library program remained firmly entrenched firmly in the 1950s? I hear too often of librarians who refuse to accept that information is often best found and shared in electronic formats. That cling desperately to their "literature" roots without acknowledging the new roles in information literacy and technology infusion in schools. That do not accept that today's learners are a different breed of cat with new learning styles and needs. And finally, that do not realize that in today's "value-added" economy it is their interpersonal skills as much as their technical skills that will make them a valued, indispensable part of their schools.

A favorite professor of mine displayed this sign on his office door. "Change or die." Succinct, terrifying, and true. School libraries must change along with (or ahead of) their school systems or go the way of the buggy whip. Or make that the card catalog.

Yet it is also undeniable that change brings excitement and discovery and joy with it as well. As JFK once said, "The Chinese use two brush strokes to write the word 'crisis.' One brush stroke stands for danger; the other for opportunity. In a crisis, be aware of the danger—but recognize the opportunity" (speech in Indianapolis, April 12, 1959). I don't know about you, but it would be a cold day in Minnesota before

I'd want to go back to wooden card catalogs, the *Readers Guide to Periodical Literature,* typewriters and lectures without PowerPoint. Well, maybe that last example is the one that proves the rule. For those of who may have a touch of ADD, the fact that one can seldom be bored and terrified at the same time is a blessing. For thrill junkies, change is wonderful.

Like a good roller coaster, change is at the same time both exhilarating and frightening. On reflection, I am glad these columns demand a positive attitude toward transition.

What other choice do we have?

On Professional Skills and Dispositions

Praise for Media Specialists Who ...

June 1995

- Only read the newspaper in the lounge.

- Don't publish overdue lists.

- Read with a pencil in hand.

- Always find a book "just like the last one."

- Rescue lost computer files.

- Are active members of their professional organizations.

- Exemplify the tenets of intellectual freedom and copyright.

- Keep learning.

- Give up a lunch hour to track down a reference question.

- Write and phone their legislators.

- Lead the way in inclusive education.

- Always give kids the benefit of the doubt on whether book has been returned.

- Have mastered skills not yet invented when last in college.

- Give you a lift when you break down on the Information Super Highway.

- Remember libraries are the only place some children feel comfortable in school.

- Teach how to make hanging indents in a word processor.

- Serve on deadly dull curriculum meetings after school.

- Volunteer at the public library or food shelf or conference committee.

- Serve on new building planning committees.

- Buy posters from personal funds.

- Say "anything's possible," rather than "no."

- Don't charge overdue fines.

- Have found a way to somehow serve every teacher on staff.

- Use "voices" when they read, and let children act out *Three Billy Goats Gruff.*

- Don't agree with everything they read in professional journals.

- Encourage students to use the drawing and painting programs on the computer.
- Have their libraries open both the first and last days of school.
- Don't hesitate to privately confront the principal about bad policy.
- Attend professional conferences, in and out of the field.
- Recommend Roald Dahl and fight to keep books about ghosts and witches.
- Make the world richer for nearly everyone with whom they work.

Boy, am I lucky to know and work with librarians like these!

How We Spend Our Days

November 1996

Time management is a big business these days. Stephen Covey admonishes us to "put first things first" (Covey 1990). (If I could just find the time to read it.) The local Franklin store sells us ever larger and more complex calendar address book/notebook/goal setting/to-do-list/project planners all wrapped in genuine calfskin—guaranteed to organize our lives. (Now where did I put my pen?) Every week brings another seminar offer promising to help us reach our objectives, prioritize our priorities and eke at least 26 hours of work from every 24-hour day. (But I have conflicts every day the seminar is offered.)

All educators, especially those involved in libraries and technology, are stressed by ever increasing job demands. Ironically, our very successes have increased our workload. Convincing every teacher to do resource-based units means more time spent planning; creating an inviting atmosphere in the library means more time helping students; lowering the student-to-computer ratio means more time trouble-shooting equipment; learning to administer the network means time maintaining passwords and making back-ups; and creating that school Web site means time keeping it updated. Some days I wonder what I did with all my spare time before there was technology.

A pundit once observed that no one on his deathbed ever wishes he'd spent more time at work. Operating then under the assumption that most of us would like both to be responsible educators and have a life outside of school, we have to make tough decisions about how we spend our discretionary time. Here are some things you might consider when ranking the items on your to-do list:

Should someone else be doing this task? As a taxpayer, I hate seeing a professional educator get paid a professional salary to install software, fix a printer, check out books, or babysit with videos. When no one else is available to do an essential clerical, technical, or paraprofessional task, the professional often winds up doing it. If the professional spends too high a percent of her day on these tasks, guess what? The position gets "right-sized."

I would rather manage two libraries or technology programs each with a good support staff than try to manage a single program alone. Consider it.

Am I operating out of tradition rather than necessity? Yearly inventories. Weekly overdue notices. Shelf lists. Seasonal bulletin boards. Daily equipment check out. State reports. Skip doing a task for an entire year and see if anyone really notices. When you're asked for numbers, estimate. A job not worth doing is not worth doing well.

Is this a task that calls for unique professional abilities? Computers are wonderful devices, but even the most powerful can't evaluate good materials, comfort a child, inspire a learner, write an imaginative lesson, or try a new way of doing things. If you can be replaced by a computer, you should be. I hope every task you do each day—from helping a child find a good book to planning a districtwide technology in-service—taps your creativity and wisdom.

Teachers and principals are wonderful people, but you should spend your time doing what they don't have the training, temperament, or skills to do. What is it that you understand about information use that makes you a valuable resource? What productivity software do you know better than anyone else in the school? What communication, leadership, or organizational skills do you bring to a project that really get things moving? Ask yourself what it is that only you can do or that you can do better that anyone else in your organization and spend as much of your day doing it as possible.

Is this a job that will have a long-term effect? In a management class I teach, an interesting discussion revolves around whether a professional should help an unscheduled group of students find research materials, even if it means skipping an important social studies curriculum meeting. It is in our nature to help those who seek our help, and that's exactly as it should be. But too often, the minutia of the job pin us down, like Gulliver trapped by the Lilliputians, and we make small progress toward major accomplishments. Remind yourself that that the big projects you work on often have more impact on your students and staff than the little attentions paid to them. Spend at least one part of every day on the big stuff.

All these suggestions are easy to say, but difficult to practice. But it is important to our patrons, our organizations, and to ourselves that on a daily basis we consciously evaluate how we direct our energies. As Annie Dillard reminds us, "How we spend our days is, of course, how we spend our lives." Put that on the cover of your DayTimer.

Librarians Are from Venus; Technologists Are from Mars

May 1998

While it has not quite reached the proportions of the famous feuds between the cattle ranchers and sheepherders, there is definitely tension in many schools between the librarians and the technologists. In case you need help, I've developed a short field guide to help you tell the difference between the species:

	Librarians	Technologists
Gender	Female	Male
Background	Frustrated English teacher	Frustrated math teacher
Reason for entering field	Likes books and quiet places	Likes gadgets and quiet places
Hairstyle	Hair in bun	Hair in ponytail
Eyewear	Cat's eye glasses (neck chain optional)	Horn rim glasses (tape optional)
Accessories	Pins and scarves with book motif	Pocket protector that holds small screwdriver
When asked for help	Hovers	Hides
When opposed	Whines	Sulks
When presented with technology problem	Always blames the equipment	Always blames the user
Most often seen by others	Cataloging, reshelving, stamping, shushing	Fixing, carrying, wiring, muttering
Seen by administrators	Replaceable by clerk	Replaceable by technician

I expect you can add to this brief, facetious list. The folks I've known on whom these descriptions are based are rapidly disappearing from schools. In some cases, their places aren't going to be refilled. Classroom teachers, clerks, technicians, or contracted services are doing the daily work that they once did just to keep libraries open and computers working. These kinds of schools are usually cold, benighted places where small children sit in stock-still straight lines, waiting in quiet desperation for the next set of worksheets or computer drills. There is little progress being made toward making them places where more children are being taught more important skills in more effective ways.

But in other more enlightened schools, a new professional has arisen. Education has not yet established a commonly agreed upon name for this hybrid breed, which has taken the best, most professional tasks from the practices of library science and technology. But I've seen these folks in action. For the sake of this little piece, let's use the name "Educator X." A field guide for this rare bird might read:

	Educator X
Gender	Equally divided between males and females.
Background	Librarian, technologist, or classroom teacher who has the confidence and commitment to grow and learn.
Reasons for entering field	Wanting to help students and teachers by improving education. Fascination with information and its uses in all formats.
Accessories	Professional journals, professional network, and competence in technology use.
When asked for help	Teaches.
When opposed	Asks questions, builds consensus, and adheres to principles.
When presented with technology problem	Looks for root cause and long-term solutions.
Most often seen by others	Teaching teachers or team teaching in the classroom.
Seen by administrators	As leader and indispensable ally in educational restructuring.
Important tasks not always seen by others	Constantly familiarizing oneself with new books, media, software, and online resources. Trying new educational strategies. Working with curriculum committees.
Finds time to get important tasks done by	Delegating duties to an adequate clerical and technical support staff.

These folks bring to the educational table critical knowledge of the issues of copyright, intellectual freedom, and information literacy. They contribute an understanding of the use and potential uses of networks, educational software, and computerized productivity tools. Educator X has a "whole school" view and works to see that information technologies are integrated into all curricular areas.

These folks don't just magically appear. They are grown or migrate to habitats that have some of these characteristics:

1. The institutions in which they work actually have a desire for change.

2. Their institutions provide Educator X with time to work and learn. That means they do not provide teacher prep time or baby-sit study halls. It means that they do not teach six classes and have an "extra" prep time to do technology or library work. Integrating information technologies into the school is their *full-time* job.

3. Educator X environments provide clerical and technical support. Books must be reshelved, software must be loaded, and equipment must be checked out if the school's daily activities are to continue. If paid support staff is not available, the professional usually winds up doing those tasks rather than the planning, teaching, and supervising ones. Fact of life.

4. These schools understand that Educator X needs staff development opportunities above and beyond those offered to the classroom teacher. Their schools find resources to send her to conferences, workshops, and planning meetings dealing not just with technology or libraries, but also assessment, graduation standards, and other areas of curricular reform with which libraries and technology might assist. Educator X then becomes the in-house support person for broad reform initiatives.

5. The people who do the hiring of all school personnel look at people skills first and technical skills second when hiring for such positions. Little things like the ability to write and speak clearly, respond to others with empathy, handle conflict, and supervise others are viewed as more important than being able to catalog a video or install a network card.

6. Schools in which Educator X thrives have high expectations of all their staff, but especially of their leaders. Their governing boards expect plans, goals, timelines, and reports. They expect clear and regular communication with parents and the public. They expect responsible, visionary leadership.

The names don't really matter much. I have known Educator X's who are called media specialists, technology directors, librarians, information specialists, computer coordinators, information literacy teachers, technology integration specialists, and teacher-librarians. Those of you who fill the Educator X role know you are. Those of you who want to become an Educator X or want to hire one know the habitats in which they thrive.

Intelligence Deficit Syndrome

November 2002

I like to think of myself as a person of at least average intelligence. But the more I use technology, the less sure of that I become. Let me give you an example.

> I purchased a new cell phone. It worked fine in the telephone company office when I bought it. I took it home and it stopped working. I took it back to the telephone company and it worked fine. I took it home and it stopped working. So I did the logical thing and left it sitting on my desk for a couple of months.
>
> But the second bill I received for services I wasn't using made me mad enough to go back yet again to the telephone company where the 20-something young lady looked at it, dialed a number with it, and sat back rather smugly as the phone on her desk rang.
>
> "Wait," I said. "Give me that." She handed it to me and I tried to dial. Nothing happened. "See!" I cried and handed it back to her, happily knowing it was my turn to be smug.
>
> It didn't last long. The lady actually stole one of my favorite lines and said, "Works better when you turn it on. Press this button first."
>
> "Look, I push that button till the cows come home. It still doesn't work," said I.
>
> "Try holding it down for a two-count like the directions say," said she. It worked and I left her office feeling dumber than dirt.

The experience exacerbated what I call my IDS—Intelligence Deficit Syndrome.

See if any of these "technologies" have given *you* IDS:

- **Having to use over 20 numbers to make a long distance telephone call.** The number string for me to dial out from a hotel using my credit card looks something like this: *9-1-800-228-8288-507-555-1234-863-037-7459-4339*. I count 36 numbers I have to remember.

- **Having a stove with burners set in a rectangular pattern and knobs set in a row.** I have to look at the little diagram beside the knob *every* time I light a burner.

- **Having one car with the wiper lever on the left side of the column and one car with the wiper level on the right side of the column.** I wipe when I want to dim, and I still haven't quite got the wash to work on a consistent basis.

- **Pushing a glass door when you should have pulled on the door.**

- **Scorching yourself because you don't know if counterclockwise makes the water in the shower hotter or colder.** This is a common hotel trauma for me.

- **Knowing what fewer than 50 percent of the buttons do on the VCR's remote control.** And I never remember how to get out of the on-screen menu. At least my deck doesn't blink 12:00, although I haven't changed the time to accommodate for daylight savings time. Let's see, is that fall back or fall forward. Damn!

- **Worrying that dragging the little disk icon on your Macintosh to the trashcan icon will erase the files on the disk.** For some users I've made an alias of the trash icon and gave it a symbol that looks like an arrow. Eases the fear.

With the possible exception of a few 18 year-olds, most of us at some time suffer from IDS.

Donald Norman (1994) argues that engineers often don't create user-friendly technologies. Non-intuitive operations (glass doors), counterintuitive controls (trashcan icons), overly complex devices (VCR remotes), or lack of consistency between devices (wiper controls), all can and should be reengineered with a little more human psychology in mind. It's not the lack of intelligence or ability on the part of the user, but poor design that leads to frustration when using technology.

So what does this have to do with school librarian, you're asking? Like many librarians, I do not have a technology background. My small competencies are in the areas of the humanities, writing, and education. I suspect many in our field share this history. But I believe that very lack of technology background makes us especially sensitive to the struggles of students and teachers who are experiencing problems using complex technologies. We have a certain empathy that most technology "experts" simply do not.

Several of the excellent librarians in our district have capitalized on their ability to empathize. When analyzing whether the problem is "on the desk or in the chair," these folks automatically assume the problem is on the desk—with the technology. Even if it *seems* like

SUD (Stupid User Dysfunction), they know that it is only poor design that keeps an otherwise bright and capable person from intuiting the proper operation. You *never* hear them say things like:

- No, the other right arrow.
- I've seen third graders who can do that better than you.
- It works better when you turn it on.

Good teachers have always known the difference between ignorance (a perfectly respectable, correctable state) and stupidity (a regrettable condition for which a cure is unlikely). An empathetic approach recognizes the difference and allows the learner to learn without feeling stupid. And that is important for both kids and adults.

Now if I can just master how to store numbers in this darn phone . . .

Getting the Job You Deserve

March 2001

There are librarians who have truly horrific jobs. I hear from them now and then. After working, pleading, planning, exhorting, team-playing, designing, and praying, they are still in positions in which it is impossible to feel like a true professional who does work that benefits kids and is personally gratifying. If you are one of those folks who has sincerely tried everything but is still working in a school culture that squashes innovation, exhibits benighted leadership, ignores any attempt at a constructivist approach to education, worships the standardized test, and fails the needs of far too many students, I say it's time too look for another job instead of beating your head against the wall—or buying lottery tickets.

This is a good time to look for a better job. Breathing teachers are in short supply, and good teachers are even scarcer. Something like 40 percent of the teaching profession is due to retire within the next five years. It's a job seekers' market. Good schools are beating the bushes for great librarians.

There are two keys to getting the job you deserve. The first is having the ability to sell yourself. That's what most folks worry about. But as a job seeker, I would also be very careful choosing the district, building, and administrator for whom I would want to work. It makes no sense to leave one unsatisfying job for another.

Let's look at both aspects of getting not just another job, but one that pays in more ways than just salary. You should know most of these strategies already:

Sell yourself.

All the standard stuff. Having a good resume, being on time for the interview, dressing professionally, and writing thank-you notes following the interview are pieces of advice any good job-seeking guide will give. Buy one and pay attention to it. I don't give anyone with a badly formatted resume an interview or a casually dressed applicant consideration for a job. Appearances won't get you a job, but they can sure keep you from getting one.

Prepare for interview questions. Do a search in the LM_NET archives for "interview questions." A surprising number of *hits* have been compiled of the usual and not so usual questions you might be asked at an interview. "Tell us something about yourself." "What are your greatest strengths and weaknesses?" "Why did you leave your last job?" are all opportunities to promote yourself, but only if you are prepared to answer them.

Tell stories that emphasize your past accomplishments. Pick your three or four best professional qualities and make sure the interview team hears specific examples of how you have applied them in previous work settings. If you are a great team player, tell about that project you and a teacher jointly designed and delivered that kids and parents are still talking about. Unless you have no work experience at all, people doing the hiring won't give a rip about where you went to school or the kinds of grades you earned. They want to hear about the wonderful *real* things you've done. Best predictor of future performance is past performance, and all that.

Portfolios sell. Shelly's interview didn't seem to be going particularly well. Like many folks, her nerves made her less than articulate. But then she pulled from her bag a three-ring binder. It held plastic-sleeved sheets of teaching materials, computer-generated artwork, samples of her former students' work, and very best of all, wonderful photographs of her working with students in happy, productive settings. She didn't have to say much. She had visible evidence of the exciting things she had done with students in her last job. And now she's doing them for us.

Being personable is everything. Kathy was a high school librarian in a local private school. When an elementary library job opened up, she asked for an interview. Although she lacked elementary teaching experience, she was given an interview along with two other more experienced candidates who looked very, very good on paper. But during the interview, Kathy's personal warmth overshadowed the experience of the others. The teachers on the committees simply said, "This is a person I would love to work with. She is calm, comforting, and capable." They were right. She is.

Find the right "buyer." So you are one hot property. How do you keep all his wonderful personal capital you have from being squandered? Find a place that is genuinely interested in what a good library program can do for kids. It is *your* job to:

Ask important questions. What do you see as the role of the library program in the school? How are departmental budgets determined? Is there a leadership team in the building and would I have a position on it? What technical, clerical, and district support can I expect? What do you envision as my most important goals in the coming year? In the next five years? Good interviews are an exchange of information, not monologues. By asking a school to sell itself to you in a non-confrontational way, you show the value you place on yourself as well.

Carefully examine the physical plant. Ask to see the library and school. It's usually evident by looking at the level of activity, age of the collection, quality of technology, and even the condition of the furniture how valued the current library program is. A shabby facility can be a great opportunity if the principal says something like, "We really need someone who can turn this place around and I am prepared to find the resources needed for you to do that." But make sure that commitment exists.

Talk to the person who last held the position. You know *your* references will be checked. You should be checking out your potential new school's references as well. Just what does the former librarian have to say? Why is he or she leaving? Talk to teachers in the building if at all possible. Compare what you hear from the interview committee, the former librarian, and teachers. Then synthesize. Ah, primary research!

Look for challenges. While a bigger paycheck never hurts, a job that offers opportunities that can provide professional satisfaction will make you happier in the long run than that extra 50 dollars per paycheck. Being appreciated by the principal, enjoying one's co-workers, having fun with the students, and actually looking forward to the next day of work makes not just a job, but a life, worth having.

While nobody has the perfect job, silk purses can't be made from sow's ears. Doing the impossible sometimes actually is impossible. If you have given your job all you can and it is turning you into someone you really don't want to be, remember the words of W. C. Fields: "If at first you don't succeed, try, try, and try again. Then give up. There's no use being a damned fool about it."

Look for school where success is possible.

Join Us

May 2002

> Ninety percent of what is known about the human brain has been discovered in the past 20 years.

I can't verify the factoid above, but it rings true. With the use of CAT scans and other technologies, the brain has become accessible in much the same way the sea became knowable once SCUBA gear was invented. And as understanding about the brain grows, doctors can change the way they treat its problems. The physician practicing medicine the same way she was taught it even 10 years ago is an outright quack.

School librarians are also practicing in powerful currents of change. Higher accountability requirements, new sources and formats of information, and new discoveries of how humans learn have led to fast and important changes in our field. And I would argue that is as important that we stay current as it is for the physician. After all, as one pundit put it, doctors can only harm one person at a time; teachers can mess up a whole class.

It can be tough to stay informed. There is just so much to learn! I've a stack two feet high of unread journals from the past couple months. I get dozens of informative e-mails and feeds I shouldn't be deleting without reading each and every day. There are dozens of books I've been meaning to get to. What's a person who works for a living supposed to do? Improving professional practice while actually practicing one's profession has been likened to changing the oil on a moving car. I agree.

There is hope. One of the most helpful and necessary things professionals in any field can do to stay informed and connected is to join their professional organizations. Really, really.

These come in basically two flavors: state and national. You can find contact information for your state's school library organization on the American Library Association Web site. For example, Minnesota's state association is the Minnesota Educational Media Organization (MEMO).

The national organization for school librarians is AASL (the American Association of School Librarians, a division of the American Library Association); IASL (the International Association of School Libraries) welcomes members from around the world; and ISTE (the International Society for Technology in Education) has a strong special interest group for school librarians—SIGMS.

I am really surprised that a higher percentage of people in our profession don't belong to either their state or national organizations, especially knowing what these groups can offer:

Communications. Most state organizations excel at this. Through newsletters, electronic mailing lists, Web sites, journals, and regional meetings, I can keep up with the important happenings around the state. It's great to have that great human database of experiences to which to turn and learn. *Knowledge Quest,* AASL's well-edited journal, presents a balance of research, best practices, and inspiration.

Legislative action. Our state organization formulates a legislative platform and hires a lobbyist to speak for us to lawmakers. We have been able to influence funding, professional certification, and statewide telecommunications projects in this way. AASL and ISTE speak on our behalf on federal education, professional standards, copyright, and information access issues.

Conferences. I'll admit it. I'm a conference junkie. Whether state or national, school library conferences are wonderful for:

- Connecting with seldom seen colleagues (Whew, I'm not the only hopelessly confused person in the world.)
- Hearing keynote speakers (Cool. New ideas—and jokes—for the teachers' lounge.)
- Attending breakout sessions (At last, practical advice for solving real problems.)
- Visiting vendors (All right! Free pens and sticky notes.)

Ongoing educational opportunities. Professional organizations are a great source for workshops, done in a physical or increasingly virtual classrooms, that can help us all survive and thrive during rapid change.

So OK, I have my problems with professional organizations too. They sometimes seem resistant to new ideas and new voices in leadership, becoming ideologically entrenched—forgetting Einstein's warning that insanity is doing the same thing over and over again and expecting different results. I question their political strategies at times. And like most people, I detest paying dues and going to meetings. But if any of these things are keeping you from joining, remember: If you can't beat them, join them. Then beat them.

My friend and fellow librarian Tom Ross of Aitkin, Minnesota, reminds us of perhaps the most important reason to join our professional organizations:

> I am struck by our need to meet with each other to willfully engage in a battle for an optimistic vision for what we do. While the struggle for improving our media programs is often political and social, it is also a battle of the mind. If we remain alone in our understanding of the gifts we share with our students, we fail to feed ourselves the vital truths that will empower us to go once more "into the breach." We spend so much time flailing against the wind that we forget to rejuvenate and that tiredness too can undermine our goals, our programs, and our best intentions for our students. How do we rebuild our vigor? By supporting each other, by taking classes where we sharpen our skills, by sharing our woes, by calling on each other, and by meeting together at conferences. (Posting to the MEMO listserv)

Tom, you're a poet. I look forward to seeing you at the fall conference!

Weed!

August 2002

I once took over a job from Evelyn, who had been a school librarian for 20 years. During her tenure, she never threw *anything* away—literally. Most of the books were of an age that they could drink. Many could and should have retired. One book had not been checked out since two weeks prior to Pearl Harbor.

The reason I can state with confidence she threw nothing out is because the bottom left drawer of her desk contained nearly a dozen years of the *Sports Illustrated* swimsuit editions in pristine condition. Happy, happy Doug!

I could just envision Evelyn's dilemma. "I can't put this out but I can't throw it away. I can't put this out but I can't throw it away. I can't put this out but I can't throw it away." It must have cost her sleepless nights.

I thought about Evelyn and weeding after reading Minnesota's recently released statewide study of its school library programs. Modeled after the Colorado and other state studies, it contains lots of interesting data. But one part of the study just jumped right out at me. The *average* copyright date of a book sitting on the shelves on our state's school libraries is 1985. Ouch.

The first article I ever wrote for professional publication appeared in *School Library Journal* way back in 1990 and was called "Weeding the Neglected Collection." It told how and why I tossed about half of the books on Evelyn's shelves. The recently released study is a clear indication that my advice to weed was ignored in the last century. So I will try again in this one.

Poorly weeded collections are not the sign of poor budgets but of poor librarianship. Period. Only two things can happen if library material replacement budgets are inadequate. The collection ages if the librarian does not weed. The collection gets smaller if the librarian does weed. That's it.

Small, but high-quality collections are infinitely better. And this is why. Continuous, thoughtful weeding:

Rids your collections of sexist, racist, and just plain inaccurate materials. And you've been complaining about the Internet being a source of bad information. Any books about the 48 states? Titles that predict that one day man will land on the moon? Tomes in which the Soviet Union is still a major political power? My favorite weeds were these:

- *Boy Electrician*
- *Boy's Book of Rifles*
- *Boy's Book of Verse*
- *Boy's Book of Great Detective Stories*
- *Boy's Book of Tools*
- *Boy's Book of Turtles and Lizards*
- *Boy's Book of King Arthur*
- *Boy's Book of Outboard Boating*

- *Boy's Book of Sherlock Holmes*
- *Boy's First Book of Radio and Television*

There was no "Girl's" book of anything, but if there had been, I'm sure it would have been of cooking, sewing, or dating.

Makes the good stuff easier to find and more appealing. Kids and more than a few adults do judge books by their covers. Publishers design bright and attractive book jackets and paperback covers for a reason. A common reason people give for not using a library is that library books are often physically dirty. Few students are willing to plow through dozens of books with nasty old worn-covered books to get to a good one. Now that I think of it, that's a pretty good reason to clean the fridge now and again too.

Sends the message that the library may not be adequately funded. If you went into your neighbor's pantry and saw the shelves filled with boxes of breakfast cereal, you'd conclude your neighbor had plenty to eat. But what if those boxes were empty? Shelves filled with books of no value are the equivalent of pantries full of empty cereal boxes. Visitors don't look very hard at book collections. They only see whether shelves are empty or full. Your budget is unlikely to increase if the perception is that you have a library full of materials already.

One very sweet librarian came up to me after I gave a talk on budgets in which I railed about weeding. "But, Doug," she said, "if I weed, my collection will be too small for the school to meet accreditation standards." My tongue-in-check advice was to replace the books with those fake books one finds in furniture stores if the standards only required quantity not quality. Whether directly stated or not, I am quite sure her accreditation standards call for usable books, not just any books in the library.

Find and read Betty Jo Buckingham and Barbara Safford's *Weeding the Library Media Collections* (1994). It's an authoritative guide that will give you confidence.

Whether fortunate or unfortunate, many people regard books as sacred objects and have difficulty throwing them away. An industrial arts teacher at Evelyn's school glares at me to this day, claiming he hurt his back climbing out of the dumpster into which I had thrown away some "perfectly good books." What he did not understand and we need to remember is that it is not books that are sacred, but the thoughts, inspiration, and accurate information they contain.

Weed! I'm not telling you again.

Librarianship as a Subversive Profession

March 2005

> Subversion: a systematic attempt to overthrow or undermine a government or political system by persons working secretly from within.
>
> *—Merriam-Webster Online*

Not long ago, I pulled my old copy of Postman and Weingartner's *Teaching as a Subversive Activity* (1969) off the bookshelf. I paid an astronomical $2.25 for a paperback copy when a college student in the early 1970s. It has lost a few pages in the introduction and first chapter. You'd think for $2.25 you'd get something that holds up better. But the book's contents are as readable and relevant today as when written at the height of the Vietnam War and civil rights movement.

Postman and Weingartner argue that schools, because of their bureaucratic natures, cannot and will not reform themselves. That learning that is irrelevant is also pointless. That standardized tests don't measure up. That schools reinforce conformity and mindless adherence to a "one right answer" mind set. And conclude that it is up to individual teachers to "subvert" practices and policies that are not in their students' and society's best interests.

While I wouldn't want this getting back to my superintendent, I have always prided myself on being a secretly subversive librarian in both small and large ways. The first time I realized my subversive nature was when I argued for new carpeting and air-conditioning when remodeling a library "to protect the computers and preserve the books" when the real reason was that these things would actually make the place more enjoyable for the *people* in the library. Hey, it worked! For a fleeting moment, I thought I might have a career in politics.

By our nature, we as librarians often say we are doing something for one reason, when deep inside we know the true reason is one that may not be acceptable to our institution.

- We order exciting books and high interest magazines and bill them as "practice reading" materials designed to improve student test scores, when our true aim is to develop a love of reading and open young minds to the beauty and wonder of literature.

- We form library advisory boards that offer us support to balance administrators who may not.

- We teach our students computer skills, not to make them "computer literate" or help them use drill and practice software, but to locate and find materials that contain reliable information and express a wide variety of opinions.

- We teach the research process, less to help students satisfy requirements in English or social studies classes, but to help them learn how to one day use information to help them answer genuine questions and solve real problems.

- We use puppets and share fairy tales just because they are so darned much fun, not primarily because they effectively transmit our cultural heritage.

- We do inter-library loan for teachers and administrator even when it is for their book groups or graduate work.

- We create and promote the use of rubrics and checklists as an antidote to multiple-guess tests and standardized testing.

- We accept the role of network administrator, controlling passwords in order to gain the same respect enjoyed by the school secretary and custodian.

- We serve on a mind-numbing number of committees, less to advance the goals of our school, but to make sure those goals are good ones.

- We teach kids not just to find information but to be skeptical of it by looking for authority and bias.

- We make sure reports that warn of the dangers of too much technology use by children like the Alliance for Children's "Tech Tonic" and "Fool's Gold" are widely read and discussed.

- We advance Postman and Weingartner's positions that the questions are as important as the answers, that there is no one right answer but many answers to most questions, and that relevance is necessary if real learning is to happen. Oh, but we call this collaboration to support the curriculum.

- Perhaps most importantly, we work to make our libraries at least one place in the school that is child-centered, safe, fun and exciting.

As terrible as the word itself sounds, subversion is not a terrible thing. In fact, it's exactly the right thing to do if what one is subverting is detrimental to children. OK, sing along with me a verse of Pikku Myy's updated lyrics to Tom Paxton's 1960s song that began Postman and Weingartner's book:

> What did you learn in school today, dear little girl of mine?
> What did you learn in school today, dear little girl of mine?
> Learning's just a job I do
> From seven thirty 'til half-past two
> And all my interests have to wait
> 'Til I drop out or graduate
> And that's what I learned in school today
> That's what I learned in school.

A Secret Weapon—Niceness

May 2005

I've learned that people will forget what you said, people will forget what you did, but people never forget how you made them feel.

—Maya Angelou

The power of being a nice person is rarely discussed in the literature, but it probably has a bigger impact on our effectiveness and job tenure than any technical or professional skill we might hone.

Off-handedly, an adjunct college professor I once had observed, "You will make mistakes on the job, so keep this in mind: People will forgive your mistakes if you are generally a nice person; they never forget them if you behave like an ass." I think of his wisdom often.

Now before you start thinking, "There goes Johnson, setting himself up as another Gandhi or something," I will admit upfront that being nice does not come naturally to me, especially at airline counters, during rush hours, or in situations with educators, parents, or students who feel no particular need to be pleasant themselves. I am convinced that behaving well is learned, not genetic. And I continually look for those who can teach me the skills that make me a person with whom others like to work.

Here are some traits I admire in others and try to cultivate personally:

Having great listening skills. This is tough for guys. We are, after all, guys. I can offer advice even before I know the dimension of the problem. But I know that hearing people out is sometimes even more important than being able to help. Harvey Mackay, a business columnist states: "You'll know you've attained your goal of being a good listener when you can utter two sentences in an hour-long conversation, and the other speaker thanks you for input and adds, 'You always have so much to say!'" That's my goal.

Being empathetic. A former principal who had been a guidance counselor had this system for dealing with people who were upset. He would paraphrase their statements and ask if what he just said was what they meant until they would respond with, "Yes, that is exactly what I mean." It was only then that he knew the other person was listening and there could be a conversation. Try it sometime—it works.

Assuming any request is possible. I love people whose automatic response to an idea is "anything is possible." Now the following conversation might involve the nitty-gritty details about while although that idea may be possible it may not be advisable or describe some of the implementation challenges. But I appreciate the positive attitude. I also like being treated as though I have a functioning brain and being given the respect of a good explanation when something can't be done. Citing "policy" does not qualify as a good explanation.

Responding in a timely manner. We coach our tech staff to always respond to e-mails and phone calls in as timely a manner as possible. Even if it is only to say, "I got your message and I will be there on _____" or "I don't know the answer to your problem, but I am working on it." Putting off responding to people never makes things better, only worse.

Looking for the win/win solution. This is still the best of Covey's *Seven Habits of Highly Effective People*. As he reminds us, a good course of action is never giving in or even compromising, but continuing to talk it over until both parties agree that the action is a win for both. Keep searching for the "third way." It is always there.

Giving the benefit of the doubt. Librarians who give kids the benefit of the doubt have a special place in my heart. The response to the assertion "I brought the book back last week" should be a trip to stacks, not a dirty look. I've found too many books that somehow failed to get to the shelf without getting checked in to suspect the veracity of any student.

Passing on compliments. The teacher, the administrator, or parent who lets me know when one of my staff did something nice for them puts the person offering the compliments on my list of nice people.

Analyzing before emoting. I've found that a short temper has never worked in my favor—ever. In fact, when somebody gets me mad, they have "won." Diligently practice the common definition of a diplomat: a person who thinks twice before saying nothing—and then tells you to go to hell in such a way that you actually look forward to the trip.

Being nice is not the same as being passive, being quiet, giving in, or staying out of the way. You can still have your beliefs, opinions, and goals. In fact you must, especially as an advocate for your students. But please remember Dr. Angelou's words that began this column. How we make children feel today will be remembered when they become teachers, principals, school board members, and taxpayers one day.

Names Can Never Hurt Me

November 2005

I have assiduously avoided entering into the "what do we call ourselves" job title discussions. Like too many arguments, they seem to generate more heat than light. Professionals I respect both love and despise certain job titles. Now, if you are expecting a simple pat answer to the job title question, just turn the page. *This* column promises only to leave you confused at a higher level.

The changing nature of our job duties and tools is causing professional nomenclature to be an issue for our profession. It's happened before. When our collections began to include multimedia materials we attempted to reflect this change by calling ourselves "media specialists" rather than "librarians"—a title then considered mired in its Latin root, *librarius*—related to books. Now with our tasks often involving technology, we are again casting around for a new name, reflecting the new change.

Job titles like "librarian" are really more symbolic than descriptive, and symbols work as much on an emotional level as a rational one. That's why the topic is hotly and endlessly debated. Symbols have different cultural meanings that are legitimate. Think of how Christians and Muslim may view a cross.

The reaction to "librarian" says a good deal more about the person with the reaction than about the title itself. As I was growing up, librarians were the wonderful people who helped me find interesting things to read, helped answer my questions, and were in charge of an environment in which I felt comfortable. Our high school had a well-respected male librarian. So I have always felt quite proud to be considered a librarian.

Yet other poor souls have had very different experiences. Librarians to them were unreasonable authority figures who demanded quiet, had anal-retentive attitudes toward "their" materials, and may have been mean or even scary. Ardelia Lortz in Stephen King's short story "The Library Policeman" exemplifies this view. In other words, many people react to "librarian" like I react to "lawyer" or "proctologist."

Complicating the matter are gender issues. "Librarian" has been associated primarily with women over the past century, especially in schools. Having no sexual orientation issues myself (I am north by northwest), that hasn't bothered me, but for some guys a more "manly" job title is important. And women have also been historically disenfranchised in society. One might ask that if we as a profession want to establish our importance in the school culture, should we be giving ourselves a title firmly associated with a powerless class? Hopefully, one would only be asking on a subconscious level since no one would ever be so sexist and misogynistic in this enlightened era.

Yet there seem to be few good alternatives to librarian as a job title—either symbolically or descriptively:

- **Technologist** conjures up taped-glasses, high-water pants, pocket protectors, a lack of social skills, and an abnormal affection for things that go beep, and de-legitimatizes our still important print resources.

- **Media specialist** is confusing since "media" is often confusing and "specialists" tend to be despised in education.

- **Library media specialist** has 21 letters and brings with it the baggage of both titles.

- **Information specialist** is a rather chilly sounding title. Today the "information specialist" is giving booktalks with puppets. Nah, I don't think so.

- **Cybrarian** is goofy and sounds like something from a Robert E. Howard pulp.

- **Chief information officer** will get you laughed out of the teachers' lounge.

- **Teacher-librarian**—well, who wants a hyphenated job title, really? Sounds like one of those blended married names. "Hi, my name's Bob Librarian and this is my wife, Mary Teacher-Librarian."

- **Library goddess, information diva, queen of stuff, and so forth . . .** whatever floats your boat.

I know almost no research about job titles, although the focus group study *A Report of Findings from Six Focus Groups with K-12 Parents, Teachers and Principals, as well as Middle and High School Students* reported a tantalizing glimpse into what such research might find:

> In terms of professional titles, "library media specialist" is a more positive and professional label than "school librarian"—especially looking to the future. "Library media specialist" brings to mind a younger, more professional computer literate person who can consult with students and teachers alike on their modern day information needs. This title also tends to make students of both genders more interested in the possibilities of the profession. (KRC Research 2003)

Maybe the perfect job title will saunter down the path one day. But I am not holding my breath. In the meantime, it's in our best interest to respect whatever moniker people prefer. Nobody likes being teased about one's name.

My dad used to say, "Call me what you want—just don't call me late for supper." I would say, "Call people what they want to be called—just make sure they are doing the right thing by kids."

HPLUKs

February 2006

Johnson's Observation on Visitors: The number of students in the library is in inverse proportion to importance of anyone visiting.

I always carry a digital camera with me when I visit school libraries. Invariably, I capture HPLUKs in action. Oh, that's *H*appy *P*roductive *L*ibrary *U*sing *K*ids. (I think I've just lost my good standing in the AAAAA—the American Association Against Acronym Abuse.) You should use your digital camera to photograph HPLUKs too, and here's why.

First, you should be the digital photography guru for your school. This seems to be one of the first and most simple technologies adopted willingly by classroom teachers. Easy to use cameras, basic editing software, and cheap color printers have allowed teachers to create personalized booklets, posters, timelines, and bulletin boards, often with pictures taken by the students themselves. When teachers are asked to "integrate technology into their curriculum," we should remember that digital photography is a simple and effective way to do this.

But all technologies, no matter how easy to learn, are even easier to learn with help. And you can provide that help if you've practiced yourself. Along with knowing the operation, settings, and downloading procedures of a digital camera, it doesn't hurt to learn some basic principles of visual literacy—or at least, the qualities that make a photograph a good photograph. Just as we can't just teach a word processing program and ignore writing skills, we can't teach kids how to use a camera but ignore visual composition and editing techniques.

But another use of digital photography is also important. As the "observation" that begins this column suggests, it's rare that there are others present when the really magical moments happen in our libraries. Who hasn't said, "If only _____ [parents, the principal, the school board, legislators, etc.] could see this, they would support my library program!" With a camera and a little cleverness, those important decision-making people can see how kids benefit from having a good library program.

I like the ways our clever librarians in the district use digital photography. They use pictures of HPLUKs to:

- promote reading by creating personalized "READ" posters of both kids and the role model adults in the buildings holding their favorite books

- illustrate their articles in school parent newsletters

- illustrate presentations to the school board, parent-teacher organizations, and community groups

When using pictures of students, we should consider their privacy rights. One should either make sure we have parental consent forms on file or run the pictures through an artistic filter in a photo editing program so that students are unrecognizable.

Influence guru Gary Hartzell reminds us that a person's proximity to a happy event creates in the mind of the observer an association of that person with happiness. (Go to any award ceremony in your school, even if you have had nothing to do with giving or receiving the award.) Pictures of HPLUKs in your communications, I'm convinced, also create that association. Your talk or newsletter article can be dry as dirt, but if it is illustrated with HPLUKs, the audience or reader will form a connection between you and happy children.

Get your cameras out! Always remember, there are more visual learners than meet the eye.

A Trick Question

February 2007

At last spring's interviews for our new high school librarian, the stumper question was:

> How will you demonstrate that the library program is having a positive impact on student achievement in the school?

How did that nasty little question get in there with "Tell us a little about yourself" and "Describe a successful lesson you've taught"? Now *those* questions most of us could answer with one frontal lobe tied behind our cerebellums.

Given the increased emphasis on accountability and data-driven practices, it's a question all of us, librarians and technologists alike, need to be ready to answer—even if we are not looking for a new job or don't want to be in the position of needing to look for one.

While I would never be quick enough to have said this without knowing the question was coming, I believe the best response to the question would be another question: "How does your school measure student achievement now?"

If the answer was simply, "Our school measures student achievement by standardized or state test scores," I would then reply,

> There *is* an empirical way of determining whether the library program is having an impact on such scores, but I don't think you'd really want to run such a study. Here's why:
>
> - Are you willing to have a significant portion of your students and teachers go without library services and resources as part of a control group?
>
> - Are you willing to wait three to four years for reliable longitudinal data?
>
> - Are you willing to measure only those students who are here their entire educational careers?
>
> - Are you willing to change nothing else in the school to eliminate all other factors that might influence test scores?
>
> - Will the groups we analyze be large enough to be considered statistically significant?
>
> - Are you willing to provide the statistical and research expertise needed to make the study valid?

No school I know of has the will to run such as study.

If the interviewer's answer to the question "How does your school measure student achievement?" was more complex ("We look at a variety of variables that indicate learning and student success such as the successful completion of rigorous course work, authentically assessed mastery of problem solving skills, reports of post-secondary success by graduates, successful participation in extra-curricular activities, high graduation rates, and alumni and employer satisfaction surveys."), then my response could not be so flip.

How can we as a profession hold ourselves accountable in an education environment in which an empirical means to demonstrate our value is impractical if not impossible?

Joyce Valenza's exemplary "End of Year" report is one example of how to demonstrate a program's and the program director's impact on student and school success (Valenza n.d.). I am willing to bet real money that Joyce's position will never be cut so long as she is in it.

Joyce is probably among the half dozen smartest and hardest working people in all library-land. Nobody should be expected to create a report as good as hers. *But* we can all borrow some really good ideas from her report. It's organized by Highlights, Curriculum, Class Visits and Usage Patterns, About the Collection, About Service, Feedback, Staff and Hours, Additional Activities, and The Community and Beyond. She also includes information about her own professional growth and professional accomplishments.

Read just an except from the section on curriculum:

> We continued to develop mini-lessons and scaffolding to address specific learning needs. Lessons included work on synthesis of content and effective note taking. I worked closely with our seniors, introducing them to a wide scope of resources for their individual projects and assessing all of their preliminary works cited lists. I worked behind the scenes with nearly all the seniors as research consultant and as their last-minute technical advisor prior to their presentations . . .

I especially like her idea of exit interviews with seniors. (OK, making videos is rather over-achieving, but regular interviews or a survey is do-able.)

How will you demonstrate that the library program is having a positive impact on student achievement in the school?

Think about it. I bet you'll be asked in the near future. How will you answer? It really isn't a trick question after all.

Perceptions

April 2008

> O would some power the giftie gie us to see ourselves as others see us.
>
> —Robert Burns

Not long ago librarian Tere posted to LM_NET that she was "caught" reading during the school day. Her co-workers reactions?

> Well you would have thought I was lying down taking a nap. Everybody that walked by my door . . . made a comment. "I'm going to give you a

job." "If you've got time to read, I've got something for you to do." etc. Next time, I'm going to go hide behind the stacks to read!

Another LMS, Allan, soon posted an interesting reaction:

> I don't give a hoot what people think of me or what I am doing. When I have received a remark about "wouldn't it be nice if . . . . [one could read on the job]?" I have responded. "Yes it is very nice." If I am feeling a little nasty or don't like the tone of the remark, I have responded "I would be more than happy to get you some information about a library school . . ."

While many of us have probably wished we could say these sorts of things, we don't. And for some good reasons including job security and our concern about how others view our profession.

Mark's views differ from Allan's remarkably:

> I made it a point to always be busy, to be seen to be doing something. (It was NEVER of case of having to find something to do, it was a case of which job was most pressing.) I did this because its the kind of person I am, but also because of the extremely negative comments I heard about a predecessor of mine who was often seen reading the newspaper or a book, "on the job." Sadly, the general public or faculty will never understand that keeping up with current events, what's new and valuable in literature, nonfiction, professional journals, etc. is part of the job. Their view will always be 'I never have time to take a breath. How come he can sit and read all day?' or 'We didn't get a raise this year and we're short a math teacher . . . and we pay him to sit and read?' Now, imagine those thoughts in an administrator's head.

My personal rules about on the job reading have been to read only at my desk (no slouching in the bean bag chairs), read always with a pen and paper my hand, and read only materials directly related to my job. I also thought it important to be seen reading when I could be a role model, such as during Sustained Silent Reading time. I was also *very* careful never to be seen leaving my building at the end of the day without a bag o' work—just like the other teachers.

It's a sad world where *reading* equals *slacking*. But given the lack of respect society shows for professional growth and reflective practice of educators, it isn't all that surprising.

Although the librarian is among the hardest working professionals in a building, she has one of the few positions in schools with discretionary resources—time, budgets, and tasks—so therefore needs to be transparent about how she "spends" all those resources, especially time. Transparency is the only way one can combat misperceptions about our jobs.

So how can one add transparency and improve others' perception of our jobs?

1. Talk about what you do in the teachers' lounge at break and lunch time. And yes, you should be taking breaks and lunch. Talk about what you are doing at staff meetings and before and after school. No hiding your light under a bushel.

2. Send out a regular newsletter to your staff about the neat things you are doing with classes and teachers, new resources, and handy hints. If teachers don't seem to be reading it, try Alice Yucht's technique of taping the newsletter to back of the stall door in the faculty restroom. She calls this her "toilet paper."

3. Track the use of your resources and send summaries to your staff. Let people know circulation figures, numbers of kids using the library, how many lessons taught, Web quests created, booktalks given, and new materials processed. Don't just share this with your principal—let the whole staff know.

4. Try documenting student skill attainment using evidence-based practice techniques. What did the kids learn? What were the assessment tools used? What did you learn as a result? Share your findings at staff meetings.

5. Share how you spend your budget and solicit input for acquisitions. Nothing like a clear accounting using a spreadsheet to let others know that you are spending resources to support *their* goals.

We all need to work with the understanding that perceptions are as important as reality in our profession. And how we as individuals are perceived is how our whole profession is viewed.

I suppose I should stop reflecting with my eyes closed—it might be perceived as napping. Darned perceptions!

Constructive Criticism

February 2009

To avoid criticism do nothing, say nothing, be nothing.

—Elbert Hubbard

My guess is that you've made some changes this year in your library—changes that you believe to be in the best interest of kids, parents, or staff. I'm also guessing that these changes were not universally appreciated. Were a few of those people not liking the changes *more* than happy to let you know what an idiotic incompetent you are?

Never underestimate the importance of being able to deal effectively with criticism if you are to be a change agent.

This year my district's teachers' first workshop day was spent learning to use a new student information system. The implementation of big systems always include some, ahem, surprises, and of course, new ways of doing familiar tasks. Not everyone was happy and more than a few staff members let me know that I was the source of that misery.

I take heart in knowing that by the time you read this, a few months after my writing it, teachers will be happy we made the change. It is a more powerful system that is more reliable and easier to use.

Changing computer programs is akin to moving to a new house. For the first few weeks, when you can't find the light switches or where you put the screwdriver, you wonder, "What was I thinking moving to this new place?" But in short order, the layout becomes familiar and you appreciate the reasons for moving—bigger garage, nicer yard, and more bedrooms. The light switch location isn't a big deal anymore.

But last fall I needed a pretty tough hide since the criticism flowed freely.

In situations where changes I've instituted are not immediately appreciated, I joke that I need to wear my "iron underwear" since everyone wants to take a bite out of my butt. But when it comes to criticism, a thick skin is much better than armor. Not all criticism ought to be deflected—some should sink in if one is to become a more effective and just plain better person.

I see the following "flavors" of criticism directed toward me regularly:

- **Venting.** "I am too busy." "I already have too much work to do." "This means learning something new and I am about to retire." "I am frustrated with my finances, my marriage, my own kids, or my health [but you are a convenient target]." This is venting. I tolerate little of it from anyone but my wife. If I feel another person is just venting, I will interrupt and simply say, "What exactly are you asking me to do?" If the person can't articulate any solution other than inventing a time machine or changing human nature, I try to kindly say that it's not my job to listen to problems I can't do anything about.

- **Criticisms about a policy or product.** When we switched our Web hosting from a regular Web server to a content management system, 98 percent of our staff was happy and empowered. But for a few teachers who had learned HTML and had used it to create some extensive, useful, and often beautiful Web pages, the new system looked like a step backward. I found dealing with these criticisms difficult because I could appreciate the disruptive nature of the change for these few people. About all one can do is offer a cogent rationale for why the change was made. Oh, and *not* pass the buck and blame others for the choices made.

- **Constructive criticism.** I admit that I've done plenty of bone-headed things for which I deserve criticism. The first year we installed ceiling-mounted projectors in the district, I didn't think to include our custodial staff in the planning. These building-proud people let me know just exactly what a stupid oversight I had made. It was justifiable criticism and I learned from it. The person who can set aside defensiveness and actually use complaints to design better ways to do things has turned a criticism into a benefit. But it is harder than it seems.

This last kind of criticism is why a "thick skin" through which some jabs can be absorbed is better than "iron underwear" off which every complaint, valid or not, is simply deflected.

All of us are sensitive to criticism. What helps deflect the arrows is faith that what you are doing is in the best interest of others. Or as the Blues Brothers put it: ". . . a mission from God." Without this faith in yourself and what you do, it won't take much to turn you back.

You can't let criticism stop you from doing what you *know* is right for your students and your school. Reflect, refocus, and keep moving ahead.

Reflection

> Be kind, for everyone you meet is fighting a hard battle.
>
> —Plato

One of those little factoids, the source for which I have long forgotten and never been able to find again, is that only five percent of people are fired for lack of technical skills. Everyone else is let go because of "personality conflicts." (To the first person to send me an authoritative reference to these statistics I will personally send a free copy of this book.)

Folks, we all know that it's not just what you do but how you go about doing it. "Disposition" we call this when it comes to student learning. Can you not only complete a task, but do it with an attitude and perspective that is positive? Do you display perseverance? Do you keep an open mind about issues? Can you communicate persuasively without being combative? How are those old "interpersonal" skills? Do people feel better or worse after a conversation with you?

Now I wish I could personally say that I have become the master of all these dispositions. With the possible exception of Mother Teresa, becoming both a competent *and* likeable person is a life-long endeavor. And for some of us, me included, this is more challenging than it is for others who seem "dispositionly gifted." But it is something on which we should be consciously working.

These skills have suddenly taken on a new urgency. In an era where more information can be accessed anywhere from a $200 iPod and wireless connection than is contained in even the best print collection, our "value-added" services come as much from our demeanor and attitude toward other individuals as they do from anything we learned in library school. Kids and teachers now have to come to library *because* of the librarian, not *despite* the librarian.

Ours is also a codependent profession. Without the ability to work fruitfully with our students, our teachers, our administrators, and each other, we simply cannot be effective. I see this theme work its way through all the columns in this book.

On reflection, the answer to how we improve our libraries, our schools, and ultimately our students' lives may be as simple as this: "Make one person smile everyday and you will change the world."

Note: In writing these columns over the years, I used a variety of terms to label our profession, programs, and facilities—all nice ones, of course. But for the sake of continuity, I use librarian, library, and library program throughout this book. Unless I missed a few.

CHAPTER 3

On Reading, Research, and Technology Skills

Embracing Ambiguity

May 1995

As a teacher, I can construct activities that either discourage or invite ambiguity in my classroom.

Let's say my class is studying camels. If I want predictability, I would ask my class to fill out a worksheet based on information found in a textbook or taken from my lecture. The worksheet even has exactly three blanks to match the exact information for which I'm looking from my students. Easy to correct, easy to measure, done by every student in a set amount of time. My class stays in the secure world of answers I've determined to be right or wrong.

But let's now change the assignment a little. I will narrow the topic "camel" and ask my students to answer the question, "What allows camels to survive in the desert?" This time instead of sending them to the textbook or lecture notes, they'll head to the library with a blank paper instead of a paper with blanks. Students might use print and online encyclopedias, a variety of books, the Internet, magazines, videos, and phone calls to local experts.

What happens? Some students come back with a dozen facts; some with only one or two or none. Some facts are relevant; some are not. Some kids are done in 10 minutes; some need all hour—or more. We've left "right" and "wrong" answers behind, and responses now are subject to interpretation, evaluation, and categorization. Now who decides what constitutes a correct answer? Hopefully, it's not the text nor teacher, but the students themselves as a result of discussion.

It takes a special teacher to create a classroom like the second one that doesn't just accept ambiguity and the open-ended discussion it engenders, but embraces it. Some of us have been lucky enough to have had those teachers. Their discussions may have been about the interpretation of poem, an incident in history, or a contradiction in science, and they didn't end when the bell rang—excited students carried the talk into the hallways, lunchrooms, and all the way home on the bus.

Why are these resource-based, higher-level thinking type activities important? We only have to ask ourselves what kinds of learning most closely resemble those faced by adults.

When I speak to the Lions or Rotary, I ask adults about the last time they needed to learn something—the features of a new phone system, the selection of a political candidate, or even a new exercise regime. They mention reading books, talking to experts, studying magazines, even searching online sources, but they never once mention a textbook. I can't remember the last time I went to a textbook or professional teacher when I needed to learn something either. Shouldn't schools be giving kids the same kinds of learning experiences they'll be encountering outside of school?

So how do we encourage teachers and students to accept and even welcome ambiguity as a part of the teaching/learning process? This may not be as easy as it would seem. Teachers teach the way they themselves were taught. Principals place high value on ordered class-rooms. School time is constructed of small rigid blocks. Libraries are often far away, and telephones and computer networks are by no means the rule in most K-12 classrooms.

This issue certainly doesn't have an easy solution, but any solution will have a librarian at the heart of it. A librarian who models activities that may have a variety of outcomes encourages and cooperates with teachers who love discussion and ambiguity, and provides current, relevant resources for student research and problem solving.

Copy, Paste, Plagiarize

January 1996

Online encyclopedias, full-text magazine indexes, and other digital information sources have developed a bad reputation among certain teachers and librarians.

It's not that the information contained in these electronic tools is inferior to that found in their print cousins, but that students—who are often more computer literate than their teachers—have little difficulty copying big chunks of text from these resources and pasting them directly into their word processed reports. And some, of course, submit the work to the teacher as original.

The old educational specter of plagiarism comes at the speed of light to the digital age.

In the good-old purely-print-pencil-and-paper days, the teacher or librarian often had the luxury of monitoring students as they took notes by hand from books and magazines. Notes were often a required part of the research assignment.

Today it's rather heartless to ask the student researcher to sit at a computer and convert those digits already dancing on the screen to graphite and paper, and then laboriously keystroke, letter by letter, and change the analog paper-bound information back into word processing digits. I certainly can't imagine any professional researcher using such a kludgey method of gathering and processing data. In fact, anyone who deals with lots of information and has a computer knows that once text or graphics or sound or video is in its wonderfully malleable digital form, you'll do just about anything to keep it that way. That's why I hate the fax machine, but love e-mail attachments.

So how can we discourage electronic plagiarism?

Carol Tilley from Danville, Indiana, asked that question on LM_NET. She categorized the solutions librarians from around the country suggested like this:

- Instruct teachers and students on ethics in information.

- Require students to hand in copies of printouts used in a research assignment.

- Change the nature of the research assignment to utilize a higher level of thinking skills.

Instruction on copyright and intellectual ethics *does* need to be ongoing for both students and teachers. Unfortunately knowing what is right is too often not enough.

Handing in printouts, as Carol suggests, is a temporary fix, and encourages students' perceptions that they are not to be trusted.

The most effective means of preventing plagiarism involves educating teachers that an effective research assignment requires original reasoning by the student. Research that is simply "about" a topic leads to copying. But activities and tasks that ask for conclusions, ask for answers to interesting questions, ask for comparisons, ask for solutions to problems, ask for points of view all lead to original writing. These kinds of assignments help kids narrow a topic, focus effort, and call for higher level thinking. They might, heaven help us, even be interesting and meaningful to the student.

If a teacher asks me to just write "about" bats, heck, I'll copy that report right out of World Book, electronic or print. In fact, I'd encourage my fourth-grade son to take the encyclopedia page that is "about" a topic back to the teacher, and innocently suggest that someone else has already done the assignment.

But if instead that teacher asks me to

- find out if people could use the same techniques bats use to fly at night
- show how bats are like or unlike other mammals
- build a bat house and explain its design
- create an appeal to prevent people from killing bats
- write a story from a bat's point of view, or
- speculate about why are people afraid of bats

you'll see work from me which almost has to be original!

Don't blame kids for using plagiarism to keep from having to reinvent a boring wheel. If you want some originality and creativity, you gotta ask for it.

The Changing Face of School Research

March 1977

Consider these research assignments:

- High school students trace the history of buildings on their town's main street.
- A middle school class researches and recommends a location for the new city landfill.
- Elementary students collect holiday customs celebrated by students from around the world using electronic mail and the Internet.

These projects are not unusual. Notice any qualities these assignments have in common? I can think of three, and these very qualities make the projects both powerful and potentially frustrating. They are also qualities that will ask librarians to *again* rethink their roles as information specialists.

1. **Increasingly, research focuses on topics of local significance.**
   Whether researching a building, person, ethnic group, or custom, the emphasis is on things in the student's immediate geographic

area, if not in their own household. Even when the topic is of national or international scope (pollution, the global economy, the war du jour, technology, or health issues), teachers are asking students to assess the impact of policies and events on their own families and communities.

2. **As a result, researchers are being asked to use primary rather than secondary resources.** Local history is scanty in most school libraries, and when it does exist, like in back issues of the local newspaper, it's not often indexed. The county courthouse, a local university, original surveys, government statistics, and the memories of local "experts" are examples of primary information sources in increasingly common use.

3. **Each of the examples above is purposely designed to be meaningful to the student researcher.** The issues of recycling and pollution become relevant and exciting when the new landfill might be located next door to one's own house or favorite recreation area. The genuine voices of another culture's students of a similar age speak louder than any text or reference book.

So is there still a place for the school librarian as research become primary-source based? When the school's collection is not adequate or relevant to the task at hand, what does the "information specialist" contribute?

Quite a bit, actually. The tasks of the information process, regardless of the source of the information, remain pretty much the same. Students still need to formulate good questions and identify the needed information. They still need a method of gathering, recording, organizing, and analyzing the information whether those tasks are accomplished with paper and pencil, video camera, database, or e-mail. More than has ever been the case with secondary information sources, the primary data needs to be critically evaluated. One of our local student felt she had hit the jackpot when she found a woman on the Internet who was willing to share her adventures as a fighter pilot in Vietnam. She later discovered through other research that there were no female fighter pilots involved in that conflict.

As performance-based assessment becomes a standard means of evaluating student work, the communication of the researched findings becomes increasingly important. Students need guidance in deciding the medium and preparing the display of their findings, whether through thoughtfully crafted charts and graphs, a multi-media presentations, or Web pages.

For many teachers, who probably were not asked to do primary source research until they were in graduate school—if ever, the use of original research and the use of primary sources may be as new to them as it is to their students. Our job as information specialists may well be as much teaching the teachers good information literacy skills, as it is helping the students.

Will the reference books sit dusty on the shelves? The library catalog's monitor burn out and not be reported for months? Will our carefully made lessons on using the periodical database molder in a drawer? No more state reports or posters of African animal facts or "social problem" term papers? I hope not. As excited as I am about constructivist, hands-on, experiential teaching and learning, I also firmly believe real education demands that students learn both process and content.

And information technology will help with both.

A Work in Progress

April 1998

Word processing is usually the first, and often remains, the primary use of the computer by teachers. Teachers are writers—of worksheets, of study guides, of student comments, of curriculum guides, of letters to parents, of tests, of rubrics, of checklists, of announcements, of newsletters. You name it, we write it. Our schools operate primarily through the medium of print, and those who are successful in school—as students, teachers, or administrators—tend to be those who read, write, and speak well.

I have never lost my delight with the writing freedom the word processor has given me. I can remember from my first years of teaching the painful evenings spent typing tests on mimeograph paper, carefully removing the inverse waxy errors I'd made with a razor blade, and quietly praying the faded blue print from previous years' worksheets would last for just one more run of 90 copies. My handwriting is also bad so not typing student materials was never an option. (Plus I had to walk 10 miles to school—uphill both ways. But that's another story.)

My poor typing was in fact a disservice to my students. Each November, I'd pull that faded *Macbeth* test from my file cabinet and look through it. Spelling errors, missing words, and haphazard alignment of foils made the test harder than it needed to be for my students, but even worse were the questions that just didn't work because they were ambiguous or irrelevant. Each year I would look at that test (all nine pages, 60 odd questions) and vow to type a revision of it. And each year time would get short and I would use the old test, orally prefaced by an ever-lengthening set of corrections.

The word processor changed that. Finally I could keep the questions that worked, and only change the problematic ones. I could run a fresh mimeograph sheet through the dot matrix printer every year. And, Oh Happy Days!, I could check my words with a spelling checker. Suddenly the gross unfairness of the world judging a writer's ideas by how those ideas were spelled could be eliminated. I was liberated and I couldn't wait to start freeing up all the kids who suffered from the same problems I did. Those same feelings of empowerment also came from databases, spreadsheets, presentation programs, video editing, e-mail, searching the Web, and creating Web pages, but word processing was my first true digital love.

This early experience with the word processor taught me a few things.

First, because of the digitization of information, *everything* can be a work in progress. Unlike like my *Macbeth* test, teacher-produced materials can be easily modified and improved each time they are used. Spelling and grammar checkers can improve professional communication as well as student writing. And truly proficient computer users soon begin to take advantage of their word processor's desktop publishing features to add explanatory graphics, catchy fonts, and visual emphases. The homemade materials become indistinguishable from commercial materials. Oh, other than the small fact that they are tailor-made to meet the needs of the individual class.

This work in progress phenomenon is extending its reach. Curriculum can be continuously revised and guides along with collections of teacher-produced support materials can be published on the school's intranet and continuously updated. Student performance reports can be revised daily and shared with parents who given online access. Long-range plans can change as technologies, funding, or philosophies change.

The benefits of an organization that views itself a continuous work in progress are readily apparent, but the unfixedness can also be unsettling and challenging. Librarians have been discussing how the Web might be cataloged and sites reviewed. Finally the expression "like nailing Jell-O to the wall" makes sense. How does anyone review and catalog an information source that may change its location or content at any moment without notice? What skills do users of information need to work effectively a world of such fluid data resources? How does one keep up with the pace of change? Please let me know when you find out.

The second thing learning to use the word processor taught me was that teachers really do need to experience the power of technology on a personal level before they can successfully introduce it to students. Spreadsheets are wonderfully involving; databases can be as intriguing to build as any model; and multimedia presentations can buck up the most reluctant speaker. But it takes an enthusiastic teacher to get kids away from the computer games and drills, and into these "knowledge construction sets." That won't happen unless teachers have taken the time and made the considerable effort to learn the software and use it meet a genuine need of their own. Teachers need technology first.

Oh, the word processor gave me one last insight. It's OK to be a pretty terrible writer, so long as you are a great reviser. (Or should that read, "One can be a poor writer, but great reviser? Let's see if I eliminate that, and move this, hmmmmm.")

Getting What You Ask For

January 1999

I've discovered a great technique for getting what I want for Christmas. I describe the hoped-for gift—as precisely as possible. I've learned that by simply asking for a tie, heaven only knows what I'll receive. If I ask for a red and gray tie, my chances improve. But, if lead my daughter by the hand to the Jerry Garcia's at the local department store and "ooh" and "ah" over one or two, I am pretty sure to get something to my taste.

As educators begin to work with students on performance skills that cannot be evaluated by standard paper and pencil tests, the ability to write an assessment instrument that clearly articulates a desired quality level becomes critical. Whether in the form of a rubric, a checklist, or a benchmark, creating tools that describe what is expected of learners can help educators dramatically improve instruction.

Librarians have a leadership role in implementing these new forms of assessment. Having had experience with "project-based" learning, we can use our experiences to teach teachers effective means of evaluating performances and projects through both in-services and by modeling the assessments of joint library/classroom projects. Our librarians and teachers are becoming increasingly proficient at writing good assessment instruments. Here are some of their "secrets":

1. **Describe what you want in observable terms.** Remember the tie analogy? The more specific you can be with the indicators of quality, the easier it will be for students to determine the quality for themselves. A multimedia slideshow about a historical period might include checklist items such as:

   - the location and the years
   - proper clothing
   - correct transportation
   - tools and weapons
   - people doing their daily work
   - key events. What happened that was so important that we're still studying it today?
   - main geographical features
   - symbols (religious, job-related, or holiday) that were important to the people in your region
   - important or famous people, sayings, or documents

2. **Two strands: content and container.** Remember getting back English papers that had two grades: one for content and one for mechanics? Projects that use technology to help communicate the content really need two separate sets of assessment criteria—one for the content and one for the electronic container of that content. Whether it is a video, a slideshow, a word processed document, a desk-top published brochure, a spreadsheet, or a database, an assessment tool that describes the effective use of the container needs to be developed. Quality container criteria for the slideshow above might include:

   - a minimum of eight slides, each with a uniform background and layout style
   - easily seen and understood navigation buttons
   - a logical organization and structure for the stack
   - readable text
   - graphics, sounds, and movies used to add to the understanding of the topic

3. **Use examples of past high-quality work.** Using past student work, students need to see or read actual examples of quality. The

"critical elements," as Mankato librarian Kathy Wortel describes them, need to be listed. One of the dangers that using examples presents is that students may be tempted to copy the examples too closely. One way to prevent this is to change the assignment enough that this becomes impossible. If a research assignment looks at the attributes of effective leaders, one year ask students to choose scientists as subjects, the next year social activists. If geographic regions are being studied, questions one year can be about environmental issues, the next year about the effect of geography has on living conditions.

4. **Give criteria to the learner at the time of making the assignment.** Assessment tools need to be shared with students at the time the assignment is given, not after it is complete. That way, students have a roadmap to follow as they work on the project. The goal should be: *no surprises.* Here is the task. Here are the quality indicators. Go to it.

5. **Use the assessment tool to help guide revisions.** Professor Jean Donham reminds us that the term "assessment" has its roots in a Latin word that means "to sit down beside." One of the great philosophical differences between doing an assessment and an evaluation is that an assessment is a tool that encourages continued growth rather than simply judging a completed task. The assessment tool should be able to help students see where they are strong and where they can improve. And by using these tools while the project is in progress rather than simply when it is completed, such growth and improvement can be actively encouraged.

6. **Use multiple assessors.** The best checklists I've seen have places for input from multiple sources. The teacher, of course, should comment whether a quality indicator has been met, as should the student. The librarian can add his or her own unique perspective. Parents should be given the opportunity to review with their children the progress of their work. And in special cases, experts in either the subject of the research or the use of the media can provide insights unavailable elsewhere.

7. **Revise your tools each time they are used.** No assessment instrument is perfect the first time it is used. Criteria can be unclear. Too many indicators might restrict creativity or originality. We have found and eliminated nearly all uses of superlatives (good, better, best) in creating rubrics. The terms are empty without precise descriptors of what actually makes something "better" than something only "good." Keep your assessment tools in digital

format, a word processing document or database, for easy updating and reuse.

Writing good assessments take time, practice, and thought. And this includes not just instruments that measure student performance, but tools that measure the quality of programs and of professional performance, as well. The more experience we as educators get in articulating what we hope to get, the better chance we have of getting it. Remember Johnson's Law of Assessment: You'll only get what you want if you can describe what you want. And that applies to both Christmas ties and student performance.

Creating Fat Kids Who Don't Like to Read

September 1999

Few people stop to think that the company that pays the most usually has to.

—Dale Dauten

All books should be scary books. I don't mean they need to be frightening in the boogey-man sense of a Stephen King or an Anne Rice novel, but I like them hair-raising because they make me doubt some of my most cherished beliefs.

Alfie Kohn's classic book *Punished by Rewards* (1993) is just such a heart-stopper. In it, he argues that extrinsic motivation not only doesn't achieve long-term desired behaviors, but actually works against building those very habits and attitudes. And this includes the willingness to read independently.

Kohn, through examples and research, demonstrates how rewards can punish those who do not receive them; how rewards can rupture relationships between students and between students and teachers; how rewards ignore the reasons for a desired behavior; and how rewards can discourage risk-taking. But the single most devastating conclusion he draws from his research is that rewards can actually *discourage* desired behaviors.

Human beings, even very young ones, deduce that a task must be undesirable if it has to have some extrinsic payment for its performance, argues Kohn. He singles out the *Book-It* program that gives children pizza for reading a set number of books. He predicts such a program will create a generation of chubby children who really don't read for enjoyment. "If you've got to give me pizza to get me to read, reading must be pretty awful thing," he believes kids deduce.

Such a conclusion really flies in the face of what most of us were taught in our mainly behaviorist-based schools of educational philosophy. Gee, what motivation does the rat have to run the maze if there isn't cheese at the other end?

So what is a librarian to do? We want all kids to read and to enjoy reading independently, but know that not all of our students come with the intrinsic motivation to do so. Many of us are accustomed to using stickers, food, parties, and programs like *Accelerated Reader* (*AR*) that often link "points" earned to some kind of reward. Throw *AR* and other reading promotions out?

Before we do, let's instead look at ways programs that track, recognize, and promote student reading can be used wisely. Penny McAllister, a librarian from Tuscaloosa, Alabama, shares how she has done so:

> I am in a school in which our basic philosophy is based on Kohn's *Punished by Rewards* and yet use AR all the time very successfully, and with no prizes or other stuff that (AR) recommends. . . . As the years have gone by we have fine-tuned the use of *AR* so that the only type of "thing" we do is recognize the kids as they move from point-club to point-club. I've circulated 43,000 books to 270 kids (in the past seven months). The kids are happy and so are the teachers and parents. Parents who have left our school always remark that the thing they miss the most is that their new school doesn't encourage reading like we do.
>
> Why do we even care about point clubs? I've got several children in the 100 point club who are reading below grade level (and in special education). That means that they have read between 200 and 250 books to get there, most of them read during the school day. In another school they wouldn't have read 25 books!
>
> Please don't throw the baby out with the bathwater. AR can work well, even if you don't give out the gizmos!

Penny's remarks suggest some reasonable guidelines for using reading motivation programs like *Accelerated Reader:* As a librarian, I would ask myself:

Does my reading promotion program stress personal accomplishment and individual accomplishment? Do students have the ability to set their own reading goals? Can students at a variety of reading levels and abilities meet target goals or will only the very best readers be recognized? Are only set percentage of students recognized for their accomplishments or will all students who reach a goal be acknowledged?

Does my reading promotion program set goals that promote collaborative work? Are only individuals recognized for the amounts they have read, or can small groups or classes collaborate?

Is my reading promotion program only part of my total reading program? Do I still emphasize books, magazines, and other reading materials that may not "count" in the promotional reading program? Are my students also reading books because of hearing exciting booktalks, listening to enthusiastic peer recommendations, and being given well-constructed classroom bibliographies tied to content areas?

Is my reading promotion program available to my students for only a limited duration during the school year? Do my students get the chance to read for the sake of reading after the promotion is over, to really experience the true, intrinsic rewards that come from being lost in a story or learning interesting facts? Have I tried to determine whether my program really leads to life-long reading behaviors?

Does my reading promotion program stay away from material rewards like food, stickers, or parties? Are students or groups recognized for meeting their goals through public announcements and certificates? If I have to give out some physical reward, is it at least a book? (It's low-fat and sugar-free.)

We all want our kids to not just read, but love reading. It's one of the things that has always separated what we do a librarians from what reading teachers do. They teach them how to read; we teach them to want to read. Please read Kohn's book and design thoughtful activities that build those circulation figures for all the right reasons.

Everyday Problem Solving

January 2002

Hola.

Donde esta el retrete?

Una cerveza muy frio, por favor.

Gracias.

After two years of high school Spanish 30 years ago, that is about the extent of my remaining ability to converse with the folks in Mexico in their native tongue. Thank goodness my accent is so bad that most Spanish speakers reply in English.

It's not that Mrs. Kingfield from my high school was a poor teacher. Quite the opposite. Despite being at least 150 years old at the time, she taught our small class very well. As I remember, I even received a nice certificate for placing high on a national Spanish exam.

So what happened over the years to all that vocabulary, grammar, and pronunciation that I acquired in Mrs. Kingfield's class?

While some of my co-workers might suggest an early onset of Alzheimer's, my loss of skills was the result of lack of practice. I've not traveled extensively to any Spanish-speaking countries and my Hispanic friends are fluent English speakers. As we all know, if we don't use the skill, we lose the skill.

I am concerned that when we base our information problem solving instruction around a single giant unit or two each year, students through lack of opportunity to practice also forget all these important defining, locating, accessing, synthesizing, communicating, and evaluating skills. It's why we seem to re-teach the use of the library catalog, search engines, Web site evaluation, online periodical databases, and even word processing commands year after year to the same group of students who seem to have once grasped them.

Practicing information problem solving needs to be a daily activity for every student in our schools, not just a biennial "event."

It's easy to quickly brainstorm a whole raft of information problem solving mini-activities that can be done in either the library or classroom:

- Use the Internet to check the weather forecast and make a recommendation about dress for the next day.
- Search and report an interesting fact about the author of the next story being read by the class.
- E-mail students in another class to ask their opinions on a discussion topic.
- Recommend a movie or television show to watch the coming weekend using a critic's advice.

- Find two science articles that relate to the current science unit. Evaluate the credibility of the sources of information.

- Locate a place from a current news headline or class reading on an online map resource.

- Recommend a book to a classmate based on other books that classmate has read using the school's library catalog or an Internet source.

- Update the class Web page with interesting facts from units studied and links to related information on the Web.

- Estimate the number of calories and fat grams in the meal served in the cafeteria that day.

- Find a "quote of the day" on a specific topic and use a graphics program to illustrate and print it out.

Note that most of these tasks take fewer than 10 or 15 fifteen minutes for a skilled information searcher to complete. Each has direct relevance to the student's academic or personal life. Reporting the results of the research is informal and interesting. Most of these activities are meaningful ones that adults do as well.

Librarians can help teachers make daily information problem solving a reality for all students by:

Making sure the library resources are available throughout the school day as well as before and after school. Even libraries with a scheduled class located in a small physical space can handle small numbers of students coming in from classrooms. We need to let teachers know that these individuals are welcome at anytime even if the library is booked.

Suggesting such activities to classroom teachers. Tapping into the natural curiosity of students is a surefire way to improve not just skill attainment but classroom climate as well. Asking students to answer genuine questions shows respect for their intellect. The results are often personal and open to interpretation allowing for stimulating classroom discussion. As librarians, we should be informing and ad-vocating for such activities through both our newsletters and collegial conversations.

De-emphasizing formal research units that do not require original conclusions. The big projects that do every step of the information literacy process seem to be staple of most schools' curricula. But how accurately does this approach to dealing with information reflect how adults conduct inquiry as a part of their jobs or personal life? Most of us do little-bitty inquiry "projects" everyday. Where do I get the best price on that lawnmower? How do I install an FTP client on my computer? What's a good book on scuba diving? How should I dress for tomorrow's weather? Daily mini-lessons taking a single aspect of the inquiry process provide practice that more accurately resembles the kinds of problem solving adults actually do. Work in your curriculum committees to see if the daily approach can be substituted for the single giant research unit.

Developing a set of benchmark skills for information problem solving. It is still our job to assess the skill acquisition of each of our students. Rather than a final checklist of skills completed at the end of a large unit, students need a handy list of skills that they themselves can check off as they complete these mini-information literacy activities. Such self-assessment is not only easier on the teacher and librarian, but better for the student as well.

As a profession, let's work toward a school culture in which problems are solved and questions are answered every day, throughout the day.

!Bueno suerte!

Once Upon a Time

March 2002

As an elementary librarian for the Aramco schools in Saudi Arabia, one of my favorite students was a Nigerian boy named Chinedu. Big for his age, talkative, focused on his own agenda and relentlessly cheerful, he drove his regular classroom teachers crazy. As a result, Chinedu was often sent to the library for a little timeout for the three years I knew him.

Chinedu really was a pest. He always wanted to visit at the times I was the busiest. He needed watching—his silliness could be a real bother to everyone in the library. But he also liked work. As a result, I kept on hand a Chinedu—do list of small jobs he could work at during his frequent visits that kept him productively occupied. Things would go smoothly for weeks and then Chinedu would do something outrageous like purposely dumping the cart of books he was shelving on the floor just to see reactions. And I would go home wondering why I even bothered with him.

But late one afternoon, Chinedu reminded me of why I bothered. Out of the blue, he approached my desk, grinned, and in his melodious accent declared, "Ahh, Meester Johnson. Dees library. Eet is my hoom away from hoom." And I was reminded again that the library is often the only place in school that is comfortable for many, many students.

Personally, I like stories. I like hearing them and I like telling them. It's one of the reasons I became a librarian. And judging from the attention paid to stories and storytelling at school library conferences, lots of librarians feel the same way. And that's a good thing. As a profession, we should be paying attention to storytelling for two reasons.

The first is quite traditional. We can use our storytelling arts to turn kids on to reading and literature and learning. We like to do this and do it well. But I would add a caution.

School library programs must participate in the accountability movement. When our communities tell schools that basic skills come first, they are asking us to grow vegetables. And I worry that things like storytelling will be seen as flowers unless we can find ways to correlate our literature and language activities to improved reading scores and the like. Librarians know that kids who can read, but don't, are no better off than those who can't. We know that the more kids read and hear literature read, the better they read. We know that it takes special efforts to get some kids turned on to reading. We know that an appreciation of art and literature and divergent cultures is as important to kids as phonics and number facts. But for too many folks that is sort of mushy claptrap. In the current political climate, a strong tie needs to made between our wonderful work with stories and the purpose and effectiveness of "school."

There is a second reason we can and should hone our ability to tell stories. One skill all great salespeople have is the ability to tell compelling personal tales that illustrate the points they wish to make. It's one thing for the guy down at the Ford dealership to show a potential buyer a *Consumer Reports* study. But the real closer tells the story of how Ms. Jones buys this exact model every other year and swears each one is the best car she has ever owned. When selling our programs, our visions, and ourselves to those we wish to influence, we need to tell our stories. And we *should* be good at it!

Statistics are a wonderful thing despite 86.4 percent of them being made up. Numbers that tell of correlations between good library programs and good test scores, of circulation increases, of average ages of collections, of percentages of students mastering benchmark skills, of computer to student ratios, and of other "hard" indicators can be very influential with some decision makers. But often numbers are viewed skeptically as well. Shakespeare once wrote that the devil could cite scripture to his purpose. Today he might well observe that the devil can cite statistics as well.

Stories put a human face on numbers and concepts. Anne Frank is the face of the unimaginable horror of the Holocaust; Rosa Parks's story becomes the tale of every person affected by segregation; and Helen Keller's and Anne Sullivan's lives demonstrate the power of teaching. As librarians, we can use stories to personalize the effects of our programs. We need to share with administrators, teachers, parents, and legislators:

- How Susie after years of being turned off reading can't stop now that she found Avi's books.

- How as a librarian, you were able to help Juan to find good information about a career in genetic engineering on the Internet.

- How frustrated Mr. Lender's class was when looking for information on countries when most of the books in the library were over 15 years old.

- How excited Jamal got about his writing when he knew it would be part of a school Web site that all his relatives could read.

- How much easier it was for Mrs. Moto's class to focus their research when she and the librarian worked together to figure out how the assignment could tap into personal interests.

- How Chinedu found the library to be the one place he could feel welcome and successful in school.

We need to all tell our stories often and with passion. People will listen. Remember the words of the poet Muriel Rukeyser: "The universe is made up of stories, not of atoms."

Foiling the Language Police

November 2003

So what do these stories have in common?

- A tale set in the mountains
- A passage in which a character eats ketchup
- A story about fossils

Each of these was excluded as a test item or as a textbook reading selection. Being asked to react to a tale set in the mountains discriminates against those who live on the flatlands. Having to read about ketchup (Minnesota's state condiment) is tantamount to endorsing junk food.

Including material about fossils validates the theory of evolution. At least according to Diane Ravitch's fascinating book *The Language Police: How Pressure Groups Restrict What Students Learn* (2003).

This is self-imposed censorship by textbook and standardized test publishers caused primarily by statewide adoption of textbooks in conservative Texas and liberal California. With 80 percent of the textbook market dominated by just four publishers, the failure to have a textbook series adopted by a large state can be financially disastrous, making these publishers highly sensitive to even small pressure groups.

The right doesn't want witches and evolution; the left won't accept depictions of women in traditional roles or minorities treated in any fashion that might be construed as demeaning. Literature textbooks are routinely bowdlerized and history texts paint all cultures as having equal value, except our American culture of rapaciousness and greed. With political conservatives wanting children to read about an idealized past that never was and political liberals wanting children to read about an idealized future that may never be, distortion, dullness, and unreadability in textbooks result. This should come as no surprise to anyone who has recently read a textbook. I am only amazed that it has taken this long for someone to bring it to national attention.

The solution to these extreme censorship problems lies, Ravitch believes, in more local control of the textbook adoption process and common sense. Since my cynical side says that both of these may be more than a few years in coming, we librarians need to step up to the plate and recognize that we are indeed the front line against the Language Police. Although this may make us "language criminals," we must recommit to:

Building and maintaining good library collections with items of high interest, different points of view, and engaging writing styles. Library reading materials are the true antidotes to dumbed-down, plain vanilla, and incomplete textbooks. Students of all ages must have the chance to read compelling fiction, consider the arguments of writers with differing viewpoints, and, heaven forbid, be exposed to materials that may be historically accurate, but not politically correct by today's standards. We need to make sure our selection and reconsideration policies are current and enforced.

Keeping Internet filtering, if it is to be done, at the local level, not a state or regional one. Statewide filtering, like statewide textbook adoption, is more vulnerable to the attention of special interest groups. The farther away the decision is made from the user in the school, the more difficult it is to challenge an inappropriately blocked site and have it placed in an override list. Keeping the Internet a place where many voices can be heard should be top priority for all of us.

Supporting a variety of learning experiences and assessments of student learning. Librarian Stephanie Rosalia comments, "[Ravitch's conclusions] are an excellent argument to support authentic literature- and resource-based instruction, for which librarians are essential." In other words, it's not enough to have interesting and divergent materials on the shelves. We need to help teachers use them with students in meaningful ways. Rabble-rouser Shonda Brisco of Trinity Valley School in Fort Worth says it nicely:

> I understand that we must choose materials based upon our community standards and the needs of our students; however, we must also make certain that our history, culture, and future do not disintegrate because we want to create a vanilla environment that does not offend anyone. If we sit back and allow things to happen (textbook creation, adoption, and selection) without speaking out against things that we feel might hurt us (vanilla-coating of terms, ideas, and national problems), we deserve what the future gives us.

Our profession has always been a bastion against censorship, protecting children's rights to read the Twains, Blumes, Rowlings, and Sendacks of the publishing world. We openly question and monitor the ethics and efficacy of Internet filtering attempts. We consciously work for student access to multiple views and consider many voices on controversial topics so that evaluating and forming supported opinions can be taught. Our role as intellectual freedom fighters is more important than ever.

The Other Side of Plagiarism

September 2004

Here I am! Lil' Debbie, a senior at Big Kahuna High. I may be a little over-committed. I'm taking a full load of college-prep courses; I'm on the varsity surfing team; I'm president of the Future Teachers of America Club; I'm class treasurer; and I do volunteer work on the weekends, including teaching Sunday school to little blind children in their native Hmong language. Oh yeah, I work at Mickey D's a few hours a week because I have these unreasonable parents who expect me to pay for my car insurance, save for college, and even buy my own tongue studs. Plus there is this really cute guy in my AP Trig class on whom I'd sure like to get a better angle.

So I come home Thursday night at seven, tired from a rugged surfing practice session and I've got about four hours before I need to crash. I have some choices about how to use this time. Let's see I can . . .

- *Spend hours researching and paraphrasing to write this paper assigned by Mr. Fuddy-Duddy on the causes of the Crimean War. (Wasn't this like way back with Vietnam and Desert Storm?)*

- *Work on the assignments in my other five classes that are way more interesting and valuable.*

- *Revise my lesson for FTA on "How to Say the Pledge of Allegiance in a Really, Really Heartfelt Way."*

- *Give that cute guy in Trig a call to see if he can explain the difference between a sine and cosine to me.*

- *Fill in at work for my best friend who needs the night of to help her mother who is just came home from the hospital.*

One time at lunch, my g-friends and I were discussing some Web sites that let a person, just download term papers. Just logon, search, download, and reformat. On some sites I can even say how good a writer I am so the paper doesn't look too good for my writing abilities. I'm thinking this "short cut" on Fuddy-Duddy's paper would allow me to do some things that actually, like, have meaning and value?

Student plagiarism is an oft-discussed topic in our profession. And we are usually pretty hard-core about it. Librarian Clete Schirra eloquently expressed a not unusual sentiment on LM_NET:

> Let's face facts, cheating is wrong, the person has no honor. It is not the fault of anyone else if a student copies, cut and pastes, misappropriates or just plain steals another's information, ideas or work. The people stealing work and passing it off as their own are responsible. Let's stop coddling students and make them accountable for THEIR actions. It is an ethics matter, pure and simple.

Clete certainly makes a valid point. Extenuating circumstances should never justify an unethical action. Lil' Debbie in the too common (but admittedly exaggerated) scenario above has choices other than to cheat. She could talk to her teacher about extending the deadline for her paper. She could figure out on her own how the topic relates to current politics. She could take the class online from an instructor more in tune with adolescent developmental needs. Or, regretfully, she could choose to spend less time on the other, more worthwhile parts of her busy life.

Perhaps I am too sympathetic with the Lil' Debbies of the world. Many of our students—rich, poor, and in-between—lead lives as hectic and stressful as our own. When I hear and see some of the assignments teachers give today—those that ask for no originality, require no higher-level thinking skills, and make no attempt to be relevant to students' lives—I would posit that teachers and librarians share a portion of the blame for plagiarism. Who moi?

As educators, this is *our* ethical failing if our assignments do not help student learn necessary academic skills and necessary life-long skills. Research assignments that only reach Bloom's levels of knowledge and comprehension do neither.

Part of our professional mission should be to help classroom teachers improve the quality of their research assignments—whether they want to or not. Our training and experience give us a great working knowledge of what works and what doesn't with kids in this arena. We are leaders in moving kids away from "doing research" to kids using information in order to solve problems and answer questions.

My dad used to say, "A thing not worth doing is not worth doing well." Plagiarism is wrong, but there are situations in which it is understandable. Here's to less ethical self-righteousness, more human compassion, and better research questions that librarians can help teachers learn to develop.

Owning Our Curriculum

October 2004

Everything must degenerate into work if anything is to happen.

—Peter Drucker

Over the past 20 years or so, I have been subjected to two major attempts to "integrate" a set of skills into my content area curricula.

In the early 1980s, the state of Iowa made a serious attempt to infuse career awareness into every subject area, including my seventh grade English classes. The state was a good deal more optimistic that my students would be one day be employable than I was at the time. A "career integration specialist" was hired, we had meetings, we wrote lesson plans, and we even had a summer retreat at a local bible camp to discuss "career awareness." The camp actually kicked our young, rowdy group out before we were scheduled to end, and I still have extremely fond, though hazy, memories of the event. After a year, the grant ran out, the specialist became an assistant principal, and the career lessons were quickly pushed aside and forgotten.

The second major effort to infuse a skill set has been a push for teaching reading and writing "across the curriculum." This has been a sustained program by language arts teachers in collaboration with administrators and building teams to make sure students are practicing reading and writing skills in every class. The model has had a major impact on many districts despite it not needing a "specialist" on staff, major funding, or even bible camp retreats. Oh, and the language arts teachers have not relinquished primary responsibility for teaching basic reading and writing skills.

As librarians, we should be asking ourselves if we are following the career education model, asking classroom teachers alone to be responsible for teaching information literacy and technology skills, or the "across the curriculum" model, where *we* retain responsibility for these skills, but expect them to be practiced throughout the curriculum?

Pragmatist that I am, I see two clear reasons to emulate the "across the curriculum" model: (1) to teach all students a core set of important, life-long skills, and (2) to keep the role of librarian indispensable to the school.

In order for us to maintain primary responsibility for instruction, we must provide:

Clearly articulated information and technology curriculum and specific benchmarks. Your school should have a separate K-12 IL curriculum with clear grade level benchmarks. If your state has one, so much the better—use it. But if not, write your own based on AASL's *or* ISTE's standards. When an administrator, teacher, or parent wants to know exactly what skills you teach, you can readily show them.

Regularly scheduled learning opportunities with the librarian as the primary instructor. At the elementary level, these skills can be taught in scheduled library classes. At the secondary level, there need to be formal units in the content areas, or, heaven help us, actual "library" classes scheduled before major projects or as exploratory classes.

Means to formally assess, record, and report student attainment of skills. Teachers do not just teach and assume students have learned. They assess the learning and then report back to the learners and their parents how successful that effort has been. Grades, even if pass/fail, should be given for IL skill attainment like those given for reading and math on elementary progress reports. At the secondary level, librarians should give a grade for any "library classes" they teach as well as grades for portions of all research projects. Designing clear assessment tools are the responsibility of the librarian.

Collaborative means of integrating skills into the classroom. Every effort needs to be made to encourage teachers to give students the opportunity to practice and apply these critical skills within the content area. Co-planning and team-teaching such units are the natural follow-up to the separate classes and critical if the learned skills are to be internalized.

Recognized support of school leadership and the community. All efforts in creating and implementing the curriculum need to be done with support of the building and district leadership and teachers. If your district has a formal curriculum committee, use it as a mechanism to get these things in place. Parents, even more so than teachers, believe information and technology skills are vital to their children's success. Use their support to make the library's curriculum a priority in your school.

There are two things that must be present if a place is to be called "school"—students and teachers. You can eliminate administers and support staff. You can stop buying textbooks, computers, and desks. Even buildings are optional. But students and teachers are a must. If we own a curriculum, we *are* teachers.

Caution with Collaboration

January 2006

Collaborate: To cooperate with or willingly assist an enemy of one's country and especially an occupying force

—Merriam-Webster Online

Collaboration. Ah, the Holy Grail, Nirvana, and home run of school librarianship. Them who does are sainted; them who don't are damned. *Information Power* devotes no fewer than 10 entries in its index to "collaboration," "collaborative planning," and "collaborative teaching."

Skeptic that I am, I can't help but feel that anything this widely promoted doesn't have something wrong with it. Why, if we are falling all over ourselves to collaborate, are library positions still in jeopardy? Are we thinking hard enough about this rather vague word and its implications?

Why does this professional obsession with collaboration make me nervous?

Collaboration is too often viewed as a goal. What everyone seems to forget is that collaboration is just one means (and not always the best one) of achieving a goal, *not* the goal itself. Too many library studies say "such and such" led to greater collaboration. Big whoop. Did it lead to more measurable student learning?

Face it—there *are* downsides to working with others. It takes more time to reach decisions and get work accomplished. It takes time to find the time to work together. Not everyone likes working with others. Defining specific responsibilities is too often neglected. Team players may get undeserved credit or blame for an outcome. Some people are just a real pain in the kiester with whom to work. Genius and imagination may be dimmed through group-think timidity.

If I am a principal or teacher who worries about literacy rates, I *don't* worry about my teachers being collaborative—I worry if my staff is doing what needs to be done to raise kids' reading ability and the test scores that supposedly demonstrate that ability. Collaboration may feel all warm and fuzzy, but it also has to get the job done—period.

Collaboration can encourage codependency rather than interdependency. One of our librarians has been collaboratively teaching a unit with a teacher for nearly the past 10 years. The classroom teacher has students write stories; the librarian teaches students how to create Web pages that display the stories. It's a wonderful activity by two talented professionals. The problem? Why, after 10 years, is the classroom teacher not teaching her kids to do the Web pages, and the librarian teaming with a different teacher on a different project?

Too often our unconscious rationale for collaboration is not advancing common goals, but creating a codependence that might insure job security. (The teacher can't do this without me!) I personally have never seen this ever work. Most people dislike those on whom they feel codependent. We have more strength in the long run if we teach others how to do a thing, especially with technology, than if we simply do it for them. I've always argued we should be people who empower others rather than being the wizards who keep dark skills to ourselves.

The overarching theme of Covey's *The 7 Habits of Highly Effective People* (1990) is for people to move from dependence to independence to interdependence. Covey states that we can't achieve interdependence without being truly independent—which to me argues against the whole job retention through wizardry approach.

Collaboration doesn't make us indispensable. No matter how much the school budget shrinks, teachers still have to be hired—at least teachers who have a curriculum for which the public holds them responsible. Who is responsible for the teaching and assessment of information literacy and technology skills in your school? If it is the classroom teacher and you are "collaborating," your position can be eliminated because these skills will still be taught. Not as well, certainly, but they will be taught. See previous column. Power comes with responsibility for critical tasks, and if we alone are responsible for none of them, we have no power.

Be cautious. Collaboration is fine *if* we have a higher purpose for working together, *if* we have clearly defined roles in a project, and *if* it the most effective means of achieving a worthwhile goal. *If* . . .

The Decline of Reading

October 2006

Literary reading is on the decline, as we've known for sometime. The National Endowment for the Arts in its 2004 *Reading at Risk* report had these distressing conclusions:

- The percentage of adult Americans reading literature has dropped dramatically over the past 20 years. Fewer than half of adult Americans now read literature.

- The decline in literary reading parallels a decline in total book reading and that rate is accelerating.

- The steepest decline in literary reading is in the youngest age groups and young adults have declined from being those most likely to read literature to those least likely.

Why? Could it be:

- "Even the most intensive users of newspapers and magazines spend less time reading these publications than they do online or watching TV" (Jupiter Research, January 2006).

- "Time spent on the Internet appears to come at the expense of time spent on social activities, hobbies, reading and TV viewing" (IT & Society, Fall 2002).

- The average American child lives in a household with 2.9 televisions, 1.8 VCRs, 3.1 radios, 2.1 CD players, 1.4 video game players, and 1 computer. (NEA, 2004).

- Four out of 10 American adults turn to video games as their primary source of entertainment. (Associated Press, May 8, 2006).

- SparkNotes lets students download its short literature and content area study guides onto their cell phones or iPods so that they can read or listen to lessons.

But is a decline in "literary reading" the same as "a decline in reading"? And is this problem?

A not unusual chain of events happened one evening not long ago as I was checking my RSS feed aggregator just before going to bed. Hey, does that sound high tech or what?

1. I read Will Richardson's *Weblogg–ed* blog entry that . . .

2. Referenced David Weinberger's *Jo-Ho* blog that I read that . . .

3. Referenced Karen Schneider's *Free Range Librarian* blog that I read that . . .

4. Linked to an article she wrote for *Library Journal* on blogging ethics that I read that referenced . . .

5. "A Bloggers' Code of Ethics" on *CYBERJOURNALIST.NET* and to Michael Stephen's *Tame the Web* blog and his "The Library Blogger's Personal Protocols." Both of which I read.

My five-minute check turned into 45 minutes reading and my wife asking, "What are you doing on the computer? Having cybersex?" This was 45 minutes I would have otherwise spent reading a professional book.

It's starting to feel that I can exercise about the same degree of control over spontaneous online reading that I have over my caramel corn consumption—I can't stop once I've started. And I am seriously wondering how my own personal reading time is best spent—snacking on blogs or feasting on books when I have time to do but one or the other.

I'm pretty sure that reading a serious book is good for me. A thick book certainly makes me *look* smart when I carry it about. There is a genuine sense of accomplishment when I finish such a tome, much like a fourth grader completing a *Harry Potter.*

On the other hand, by blogging around that night, I stumbled on a relevant, important topic—blogging ethics—and after reading three short articles, I now probably know more about the topic than 95 percent of the rest of the blogging world—which I am quite sure qualifies me as an expert. And the knowledge gained will immediately guide my practice.

Alexander Pope wrote in his poem "An Essay on Criticism":

> A little learning is a dang'rous thing;
> Drink deep, or taste not the Pierian spring:
> There shallow draughts intoxicate the brain,
> And drinking largely sobers us again.

Is "a little learning" more important in a fast-paced world than "drinking deep"? Would Pope now have to write "A little learning is a ness'ry thing"? And just why would one want to be sober anyway, Mr. Pope?

Blogs of course are not the only source of "a little learning." Professor Naomi Baron worries:

> Will effortless random access [to snippets of books made available through Google Book Search] erode our collective respect for writing as a logical, linear process? Such respect matters because it undergirds modern education, which is premised on thought, evidence and analysis rather than memorization and dogma. Reading successive pages and chapters teaches us how to follow a sustained line of reasoning. (Baron 2005)

Gulp!

What exactly is our role as librarians when it comes to "book" reading—fight the tide or go with the flow? Is reading reading or should only reading books be valued?

Evaluating Collectively Created Information

January 2007

The most valuable resource on the Internet is the collective intelligence of everyone who uses it.

—James Surowiecki

As librarians, we have a special responsibility to see that our students learn to access the most relevant, most comprehensive, and most accurate information possible. AASL/AECT's 1998 *Information Literacy Standards for Student Learning* couldn't be any clearer—Standard 2: The student who is information literate evaluates information critically and competently.

In the halcyon days prior to the Internet, teaching this aspect of information literacy was fairly straightforward. We might have had students ask: What are the author's credentials? With what institution is he/she affiliated? What is the reputation of the company that published the author's book or journal article? Or more than likely, we just didn't spend a lot of time and effort teaching information evaluation skills, secure in the knowledge that the books and magazines to which our students had access had already been vetted—by us.

But of course, the Internet has given students access to, well, everything—accurate and inaccurate; timely and dated; biased and objective. As a result we've necessarily paid greater attention to information evaluation. The trouble is that we've only been having students ask the same questions to determine the reliability of information that we have in the past—basically, "Who is the author and what are her/his credentials?"

Like it or not, we are moving from a "read-only" Internet to one that is "read-write." And this presents an entirely new class of information that needs to be evaluated—the collectively created information source. For many of us who have been trained to put faith in traditional authoritative sources, collectively created information seems, at best, suspect; at worst, horrifying. An encyclopedia *anyone* can edit? Book and movie reviews *anyone* can publish? Textbooks written by *students?* A library manual written by *practicing librarians?* That sound you just heard was your old Reference I professor turning over in her grave.

Without even being aware of it, I've personally come to rely on collectively created information. I've long used *TripAdvisor's* reviews when choosing a hotel or resort. It's not that I distrust *Frommers* or *Fodors,* it's just that the reviews on *TripAdvisor* are written by real people who have actually stayed in the accommodation recently. There are usually enough reviews that a single crank or enthusiast stands out from the general consensus. If 9 of 10 people rave about service, you can reliably count on good service. I've found the *Digital Photography Review* Web site to be a reliable guide to digital cameras for a non-professional user like myself. More of us are reading book reviews submitted to *Amazon* and movie reviews at *Internet Movie Database.* These *vox populi* sources may not supplant the *New York Times Book Review* or Roger Ebert's evaluations, but they do complement them. And I often find myself in greater agreement with the *populi* than the professional critic.

Which gets us to the poster-child of collectively created information sources, *Wikipedia*. As an "information professional," I don't really want to admit that I use—and really like—*Wikipedia*. But I will defend its use for a number of reasons including the breadth of its scope, its timeliness, and its clear notification of controversial/undocumented entries.

We might, in fact, actually turn to *Wikipedia* as the model for reliable collaboratively created information sources, and use some of its attributes to create a checklist that can be used to help determine the reliability of other such sites. How are these for starters?

- Can anyone contribute or edit the source?
- Is a history of changes made available?
- Are a diversity of views, opinions, sources, and voices evident?
- Are there clear warnings that a topic may be controversial?
- Is there a process by which those who are misusing the resource can be restricted from contributing?

New Yorker columnist James Surowiecki advances a theory he calls "the wisdom of crowds." He writes:

> Under the right circumstances, groups are smarter, make better decisions and are better at solving problems than even the smartest people within them. On any one problem a few people may outperform the group. But over time collective wisdom is nearly impossible to beat. No one, you might say, knows more than everyone. (Surowiecki 2004)

This is why, Surowiecki, surmises, that the audience on the television program *Who Wants to be a Millionaire?* gets the right answer 91 percent of the time, compared to the so-called experts' 65 percent accuracy rate.

Collectively created information sources will grow in popularity and value. Wikis are allowing teachers to ask students to create their own textbooks. Joyce Valenza has challenged the library community to create the ultimate library manual at *teacherlibrarianwiki*. Jimmy Wales, creator of *Wikipedia,* has announced that he is turning his attentions to establishing collaboratively created college curricula at the *Wikiversity.*

Are we teaching our students how to evaluate this new type of information?

Nickel and Dimed

March 2007

> To succeed in today's workplace, young people need more than basic reading and math skills. They need substantial content knowledge and information technology skills; advanced thinking skills; flexibility to adapt to change; and interpersonal skills to succeed in multi-cultural, cross-functional teams.
>
> —J. Willard Marriott, Jr., Chairman and CEO,
> Marriott International, Inc.

Spring has always been the time I seem least content with being in education. I am usually pretty fed up with the antics of students, teachers, administrators, and a few parents. I am actively questioning whether I actually taught anybody anything during the year or any of my department's initiatives did anything for kids. I am worried about the next round of budget cuts.

So I always start wondering if long-haul truck driving wouldn't be a far more lucrative and rewarding way to put Spam on the table.

I just finished re-reading Barbara Ehrenreich's terrific little book *Nickel and Dimed* (2001). Middle-class writer Ehrenreich tells in a very readable, surprisingly comic style her experiences working as a minimum-wage waitress, housecleaner, nursing home attendant, and Wal-Mart clerk around the United States including a stint here in Minnesota, trying to actually live on what she made at those jobs. It was a glance into a way of life I only vaguely remember from my college days.

While I expected to read about the work being difficult and expenses impossible to meet for these low-paid, "invisible" members of our society, I *was* surprised at how demeaning the author found the working conditions themselves—describing drug and personality tests that attempt to weed out any "difficult" employees; supervisors that are suspicious, rule-bound dictators; duties that are stultifyingly repetitive; and simply the spirit sapping "dead-endedness" of the work and workers' futures. Is it possible, I asked myself while reading the book, that many employers actually *want* workers who are mindless automatons?

This certainly goes against everything I've been reading from politicians and business groups who want "world-class" school graduates whose brains, initiative, and creativity will fire the engines of economic development in a post-industrial economy. The report *Are They Really Ready to Work?* from which the opening quote was taken is survey of 400 employers across the United States (Casner-Lotto 2006). Employers cited professionalism/work ethic, oral and written communications, teamwork/collaboration, and critical thinking/problem solving as the most important skills.

Can one conclude that business and government don't want *everybody* to be all that smart—just the middle and upper classes?

So what does this have to do with school libraries and technology? In his classic book *Savage Inequalities* (1991), Jonathan Kozol concluded there are two kinds of schools in this country: those for the governors and those for the governed. Sadly, I think he is absolutely right. In which kind of school do you work:

- One that teaches kids to answer questions with a single correct answer, or one that teaches them to ask questions, especially of authorities?

- One that teaches kids to memorize factoids from textbooks, or one that teaches them to find pleasure, excitement, knowledge, and wisdom in reading the work of a variety of compelling writers?

- One that teaches kids to follow directions, or one that teaches them to be self-directed?

- One that teaches kids only the realities and limitations of life, or one that teaches and believes all people can hope, dream, and aspire to great things?

Effective libraries can be the antidotes to education's lurch to the test-crazy, standards-based, one-right-answer approach to "education." Of course attention must be paid to basic skills for all children, but unless you want your kids to only have a blue vest or a vacuum cleaner in their long-term career plans, "basic skills" are simply not enough.

Our library and technology programs that teach students not just to read, but to love to read; that ask students to listen to and judge different points of view; and that help students become effective, self-motivated problem-solvers are vital if we want our schools to be "those for the governors."

So, if you get the same spring doldrums I do, remember just how important *you* really are to the children in your charge—not just now, but for the rest of their lives.

What Gets Tested Gets Taught

April 2006

What gets measured gets done.

—Tom Peters

Why does no one seem to take teaching information and information technology literacy skills very seriously? Oh, maybe a few librarians have the true faith, but come on, who else in your district really cares about this true 21st-century skill set? Or can even define information literacy? Here's just one piece of evidence that IL/IT skills are not being taught:

> College students and high-school students preparing to enter college are sorely lacking in the skills needed to retrieve, analyze, and communicate information that is available online . . . only 13 percent of the test-takers were information literate. (Foster 2006)

To most teachers, adding "one more thing" to an already over-loaded curriculum is painful, even if information literacy is as necessary a skill in today's information age economy as the basic R's have been in the past. Yet schools that do not recognize the need for students to be able to use information and technology to solve problems and answer questions are negligent. How do we get all schools to recognize this critical skill set and give it the importance it deserves?

First, we need a single, nationally recognized set of IL/IT standards. No one—librarians, technology teachers, or classroom teachers—are well served by our current dueling professional standards. The AASL and ISTE guidelines have a good deal of overlap. Both would be stronger if combined.

Second, state and national requirement must require schools be held as accountable for teaching and assessing IL/IT standards as they are for reading, writing, and math. Yes, there is the toothless provision for "technology literacy by all eighth graders" in the current Title IIB language, but it is not being enforced.

Look, I am no great fan of federal mandates. Local control, I've always felt, is the best control. It can be argued that NCLB is more about discrediting public schools than about educating kids. But if laws like NCLB can be tools for making information and technology skills "basic skills," I am for them. It's the smart thing to do. Why?

- **Dollars will follow requirements.** If there is a lesson to be learned from NCLB, schools *will* fund educational efforts when there is the force of law behind them. While only partially funded at best, schools have anteed-up for the planning, testing, materials, and staff development needed to meet the requirements of making sure all children can read, write, and compute on at least a minimal basis. Should NCLB also recognize that information and technology literacy is so vital to our children's success that schools be held accountable for all students' mastery of it, the funds needed to make it happen will follow. And, in all schools across the country.

- **Lobbying by our professional organization can be done from a higher moral ground.** Our professional organizations are too often seen as self-serving, self-promoting. We "advocate" for technology use, for libraries, for schools. We should be advocating for students and the benefits that they will receive as a result of better technologies, better libraries, and better schools, and the result—students who are better prepared for 21st-century work.

- **More educators may get politically involved.** If ISTE and AASL lobby not just for dollars, but for standards, educators from schools that rarely, if ever, qualify for federal grants dollars might get excited about supporting us.

A mandated curriculum of IL/IT skills is not the perfect solution. Questions of funding, of equitable assessment, and of prioritizing these skills with other basic skills can and should be asked. But after 30 years of ineffectually using charm to get all educators to take this 4th R seriously, it's time to appeal to a higher power.

Building Capacity for Empathy

January 2009

A group of Toronto researchers have compiled a body of evidence showing that bookworms have exceptionally strong people skills. . . . Their years of research . . . [have] shown readers of narrative fiction scored higher on tests of empathy and social acumen than those who read nonfiction texts.

The quote above comes from a fascinating article "Socially Awkward? Hit the Books" about how reading fiction builds social skills and empathy (Haley 2008).

Most of you reading just said, "Well, duh! Haven't we known this for years?" But isn't gratifying to have our observations confirmed?

Empathy? Social acumen? Are these essential skills for surviving and thriving in today's economy? Our national associations and gurus seem to think so.

- From NETS 2007: "Students . . . develop cultural understanding and global awareness by engaging with learners of other cultures. . . . use multiple processes and diverse perspectives to explore alternative solutions."
- From AASL's Standards for the 21st Century Learner 2007: "Students will: Consider diverse and global perspectives in drawing conclusions. . . . show social responsibility by participating actively with others in learning situations and by contributing questions and ideas during group discussions."
- From Daniel Pink's book *A Whole New Mind*: Not just logic, but also EMPATHY. "What will distinguish those who thrive will be their ability to understand what makes their fellow woman or man tick, to forge relationships, and to care for others" (Pink 2006).

The unsung hero of many a successful enterprise is empathy. Understanding the needs and desires of others is critical for leaders, salesmen, politicians, lotharios, preachers, CEOs, writers, teachers, consultants . . . well, just about everybody. The better one understands others, the more effective one can meet their needs, appeal to their self-interests or, I suppose, manipulate them.

With a global economy, our empathy needs to extend beyond our next-door neighbor. Multiculturalism and global awareness simply means understanding, not necessarily accepting, the values, motives, and priorities of cultures other than those in which we grew up. Hard to believe but not everyone values lutefisk and lefse!

The question is, then, can empathy be learned—and how? Is there a small muscle somewhere in the mind or soul that can be exercised, stretched, and built that allows us to more fully place ourselves in others' shoes? Or sandals? Or moccasins? Or bare feet?

Reading fiction—especially when the setting is another culture, another time—has to be *the* best means of building empathic sensibilities. How do you understand prejudice if you are not of a group subject to discrimination? How do you know the problems faced by gays if you are straight? How does it feel to be hungry, orphaned, or terrified when you've always lived a middle-class life? By harnessing the detail, drama, emotion, and immediacy of "story," fiction informs the heart as well as the mind. And it is the heart that causes the mind to empathize.

Viewing the world through the eyes of a narrator completely unlike oneself draws into sharp detail the differences of experience, but also the similarities of the narrator and reader. And it is by linking ourselves through similarities—common human traits—that we come to know others as people, not just stereotypes.

Happily, empathy building through reading doesn't end with childhood. We adults can be just as moved—and influenced by novels. My nominees for best empathy-building novels I've read are Haddon's *The Curious Incident of the Dog in the Night-Time* (reading it left me with a better understanding of autistic children) and Hosseini's *The Kite Runner* (the author's experience of the horrors of Taliban-ruled Afghanistan and difficulties of cultural assimilation are profound.)

Unfortunately, as school budgets are stretched, school library funds that purchase quality fiction and library professionals who select and promote quality fiction are too easily axed, replaced by reading programs, specialists, and tests of basic comprehension.

Our politicians and educational leader rarely ask: if one can read but is not changed by reading, why bother? Empathy is an ability that is difficult to objectively measure. As a result, many educators simply ignore it, like they do too many affective skills. It's essential that we librarians fight for our programs and budgets.

Atticus Finch in *To Kill a Mockingbird* gave this advice to his young daughter:

> If you just learn a single trick, Scout, you'll get along a lot better with all kinds of folks. You never really understand a person until you consider things from his point of view . . . until you climb inside of his skin and walk around in it.

It's perhaps fitting that those of us who have experienced Lee's book have indeed had our quotient for empathy increased by reading it.

Reflection

What's the absolute minimum I have to do to get a passing grade in this course?

—my son

It's taken me nearly an entire career in education to figure this out, but I've come to believe:

- It's a teacher's job to make us think, not to believe.

- Learning should be engaging.

- A teacher's role is not to teach facts, but to help understand why the facts are important to the learner.

- If you are not having fun as a teacher, neither is anyone else in your class.

Both the needs of the workforce and society along with technological change force us to re-examine not only the skills our students must master but at which we must become adept ourselves.

Learning "technology skills" is the easy part. A good recipe-type hand-out serves to teach someone how to add a graphic to a slideshow. The trick is how to use these technology skills purposefully. That's why I have always been a strong proponent of integrating technology skills into an information literacy curriculum. Students are learning the technology skills as they pursue a more important learning objective—to use information to answer questions, solve problems, and communicate effectively.

The other big reason we need to re-examine what and how we teach comes from the experience I have had raising my own children. Here's the deal . . .

My daughter Carrie, who was born in 1973, went to school with a smile on her face and it really never left her face while she was in school. She was good at school and graduated from high school at the top of her class. She got her BA from the University of Minnesota—in four years—married in the nicest man in the world, and has produced the two finest grandsons anyone could ask for. (In that order—married, then grandchildren—yes!)

I loved going to Carrie's parent-teacher conferences because I learned there what a wonderful parent I was. In fact, I got to wondering what was wrong with all these other parents. Parenting was just not that hard.

That's when the gods punished my hubris. By giving me a son.

Brady was born in 1986. He was (and still is) a sweet guy. Smart, shy, creative, and never in a lick of trouble with drugs, alcohol, or girls. I think he was 20 before he actually talked to a girl. However, Brady's overriding philosophy toward school was "What is the absolute minimum I have to do in order to get by?" And sometimes Brady's idea and his teachers' idea of minimum were different. His parent-teacher conferences were, uh, interesting.

My question was and is "How could two children, both from such superior genetic stock, be so different?"

One possible explanation is that Brady falls directly into the demographic of the Net Generation. A 2008 book labeled them "the Dumbest Generation" asserting they've been made stupid by technology and pop culture. But that is just plain wrong.

Today's kids have different learning styles. And more than anything they demand relevance from school. As librarians, we must recognize this and modify our research projects and assessments. And help our teachers realize the importance of doing so as well.

We are getting more Bradys coming into our schools each year—and fewer Carries.

On reflection I find the theme is that all learning needs to be meaningful to the learner. It's not about information; it's about why the information is important to the individual.

CHAPTER 4

On Technology in Libraries

The Future of Books

April 1995

I enjoy LM_NET discussions of the impact of technology on the future of books. But I think too many of the responses gave us an "either or" scenario—we will either have books or technology. We forget that today's print book is itself a "technology."

The technology of the "book" has already seen a number of transitions: from clay to wax to papyrus to vellum to cloth to paper, stored as tablets or scrolls or folios or books, bound in horn or leather or cloth or paper. Standardized spelling, paragraphs, and punctuation are all relatively new inventions in written communication—as are hyperlinks.

Let's face it, our current paper printed books (with rare and expensive exceptions among those for children's and art's sake) are a pretty shoddy mess: rapidly disintegrating spines, greasy feeling paper, squinty print, shoddy color separation, subject to acid disintegration, easily damaged, quickly out of print, bulky to store, back breaking to move, moldy smelling, and visually dull. While I am as sentimental as the next person about the associative memories particular books evoke, I like to believe it is really the excitement of the story, the perspective of the author, or the lyricism of the language to which I am reacting. I don't remember the color of many book spines I read as a child.

Imagine opening a padded notebook bound in calfskin. It weights little, smells good, and is available in a variety of sizes. It runs on a watch battery that needs replacing once every three years, and has a solar panel like those in calculators. On one side is a softly glowing, backlit, glare free screen. My wife can sleep while I read in bed. I think my page's background would be a rich ivory color. On the other side is a small keyboard, a number of buttons and network jack.

Come across an unfamiliar word? Touch it and the glossary key to the right of the screen and a brief definition pops up. Many books will come with a picture and sound glossary. Touch the word, see the object, character, or setting.

Doodle in the margins? You bet, with a pen on the touch sensitive screen or via the keyboard on electronic sticky notes. Oh, I can search my notes as well as the text for that particularly pertinent passage. Set referenced bookmarks? Certainly.

I expect the less tradition bound will expect and use some content flexibility. Main character's name is the same as your ex's and that spoils the story? Do a little find/replace, and "Call me Ishmael" becomes "Call me Ralph." Or whatever. Set the latest Stephen King to mild, scary, or terrifying, or your Harold Robbins to suggestive, lurid, or Don't-Let-Yer-Mom-Catch-You-Reading-It! Only like happy endings? Select that version.

Nothing very "novel" here, but for us those of who are, and always will be readers, a digital future has exciting possibilities! Send me your ideas about what features your e-book should have. I'll add them to v2.0.

Note: This was published 12 years before Amazon unveiled the Kindle.

The Future of Books Revisited

May 2000

One of the best things about reading science fiction is that it helps reduce the shock of the future. These compelling stories often offer fascinating glimpses into a not terribly distant time.

First, let me qualify what kind of science fiction I'm talking about. My favorites now are not the spacemen vs. bug-eyed monsters type adventures I read during my misspent youth, but those that extrapolate from our current technologies and social conditions what we may very well soon encounter.

Jules Verne's *20,000 Leagues Under the Sea* showed how industrial technologies would one day allow us to explore inaccessible parts of our world. George Orwell's warned us in *1984* about technology's power over privacy and history. Orson Scott Card's *Ender's Game* uncannily predicted how anyone regardless of age could have a powerful political influence using the Internet. And William Gibson's *Neuromancer* offered the first glance a virtual world that could be every bit as real as a physical one.

Neal Stephenson's novel *The Diamond Age* is another one of those sci-fi books that punch us into the future. Fiona, the book's youthful heroine, is assisted through a very rough childhood by a most unusual book-like device titled *A Young Lady's Illustrated Primer.* This wonderful tool is a library and self-paced tutorial that offers her just the right skill, bit of information, or advice when needed.

Wouldn't it be nice if all our students had such a book? Heck, let's not stop at just giving our kids an e-book, but let's give them a whole e-backpack. What might such device contain? As I go shopping for my kids next Christmas, I am certainly going to look for all these features in a single unit:

An e-book. I visited this topic in the last column, "The Future of Print." With the advent of electronic paper, downloadable texts, and the ubiquity and increasing speed of the Internet to transport digitized tomes, we are now closer than ever to the e-book of my dreams. My student's e-book will contain teacher-customized textbooks, research materials, and of course the latest *Harry Potter* episode. Not only is the e-book convenient, but it eliminates the health risks associated with little bodies humping over weight book bags.

An e-notebook. The e-backpack certainly needs a means of storing notes, papers, and teacher-generated study materials. A small keyboard, microphone for voice input, and touch screen all should be available, plus a wireless port for the teacher to beam in the latest assignments and returned papers. Let's make sure all these documents can be easily and logically organized, stored and recalled when needed. Enough memory and perhaps that great fifth-grade mythology report could be used again in ninth grade. Or this could become a K-12 portfolio documenting the exploration of a series of related topics, each assignment building on the last? A constructivist's dream.

An e-organizer. Adults certainly use electronic organizers to track their hectic lives. Those appointment calendars, to-do-lists, and address books are also useful tools for kids who need to keep track of assignments, projects, practices, meetings, and orthodontist appointments. One of the kindest things we can do as educators is help our kids get and stay organized. The world is not kind to those who aren't, it seems.

An all-purpose e-card. The function of a library card, lunch ticket, petty cash, and sports pass should all be handled by the student's e-card. With the needed password—no, let's make that thumbprint—the e-card will electronically transmit the needed data to the appropriate computer at the circulation desk, admission gate, or pop machine. Get an automatic recharge through Dad's bank account each month, of course. Let's get the kind that will unlock school lockers and the backdoor at home too.

An e-communicator. Why be tied to the desk when sending or receiving e-mail? The e-backpack has to serve as a mobile communications device capable of transmitting both sound and data, including digital video. Wireless of course. Small laptop computers with their ability to send and receive data from anywhere in a classroom or library may well be a prototype. Now how do we stop students from passing notes in class? Or videoconferencing? Or do we want to stop such activities?

An e-tutor. Although Fiona in *The Diamond Age* didn't know it, her primer's power and usefulness were because the lessons were planned and monitored by a caring human mentor. My students' e-backpacks will be carrying the experience, judgment, and wisdom of as many human beings as they need. It will be the portable, student-oriented version of professional networks and it will surround the young users with caring adults who can offer thoughtful help when necessary.

So how do we keep this magical device from being lost, stolen, or left on the bus? I am not yet ready to make little Borgs of our students—no implants please! Although looking at the number of nose rings and tongue studs I see, imbedded technologies may not be that off-putting to the students themselves. Perhaps something wearable? A wristwatch type central processing unit (CPU). A holographic display, video camera, and small speaker built into eyeglasses. Perhaps the display can project a virtual keyboard as well? One day that twitchy kid in the back row may be twitchy because she's paging through *The Hobbit,* solving a chemistry problem, or drawing her friend a valentine.

I'll keep reading my science fiction novels. Michael Crichton's *Timeline* supposes quantum mechanics will one day be able to send objects through time. Hmmm, just think what that will do for interlibrary loan. The book may show up a few minutes before you actually realize you need it. Now that you know, the shock should be less when it actually happens.

Note: This was published seven years before "netbook" computers were released.

Old Folks and Technology

November 2002

There are three great questions which in life we have to ask over and over again to answer:

Is it right or wrong?

Is it true or false?

Is it beautiful or ugly?

Our education ought to help us to answer these questions.

—John Lubbock, a 19th-century astronomer

I think of those words often when I hear educators worry about kids being more adept and comfortable with technology than those of us who were growing up when the earth was still cooling.

It's hard not be humbled when a situation like this occurs as related by Monica Campana of Palm Coast, Florida, on LM_NET:

> Last month Google was blocked by our district because kids were doing image searches and actual pictures loaded on Google image search hit page that aren't blocked by our filter. Safe search in Google can be turned off by the kids. I vented, fumed, researched, e-mailed Google, but finally gave up and taught the kids how to use a few other search engines. One week later one of my seventh graders pulled me aside and whispered that we could still use <www.google.ca>—the Canadian version of Google, as of yet not blocked. I had to laugh because I should have asked the kids in the first place.

Many of us turn to those younger than us for technology help. The older I get, the more young people there are around. Funny how that works. When I need help editing a digital movie, I turn to my son. He downloads movies, burns CDs, and uses chat to visit with folks around the world. If I need help getting the networked printer to work in the office, our 20-something network coordinator is the one I ask. When her fingers fly through the control panels, they are a blur. Hands down, kids can do the technical stuff and are more comfortable with much of this stuff than I will ever be. And my VCR doesn't blink 12:00 either.

In *Growing Up Digital,* Don Tapscott (1999) calls the kids who have grown up with a mouse in their hands the Net Generation. Of these Net-Genners, he writes, "For the first time in history youth are an authority on an innovation central to society's development." I am not exactly filled with hope for the future when I think that the young, spiky blue-haired guy with more studs than a Minnesota snow tire is leading cultural change. Darn, that sounded just like something my grandfather might have said.

What I hope we don't forget is that the same great issues of education that Lubbock identifies are still with us today and are perhaps more important than ever. When our students download music, we need to be there to ask if there is a copyright question involved (right or wrong). When they find sources of information on the Internet, we need to be there to ask them if the information is credible (true or false). When they put graphics into their presentations, we need to be there to ask them if those visuals contribute to the message they are trying to get across (beautiful or ugly). I like to think the questions we can help answer are more important in the long run than "How do you create a new background on a slide?"

We need to help make sure our students not only know how to use these new electronic marvels, but use them well. A short list of tools is below with some of the sensibilities about their use with which we geezers can still help:

Some technologies	Some things with which old people can still help
Spreadsheets	Math sense, numeracy, efficiency in design
Charting and graphing software	Selecting the right graph for the right purpose
Database design	End user consideration, making valid data-driven decisions
Word processing	The writing process, organization, editing, grammar, style
Presentation software	Speaking skills, graphic design, organization, clarity
Web page design	Design, writing skills, ethical information distribution
Online research	Citation of sources, designing good questions, checking validity of data, understanding biases
Video editing	Storyboarding, copyright issues when using film clips and audio
Chatroom use/Instant messaging	Safety, courtesy, time management

No matter how sophisticated the N-Genners are technologically, in matters of ethics, aesthetics, veracity, and other important judgments, they are, after all, still green. By virtue of our training and life experiences, we can apply the standards of older technologies (the pencil, the podium, the book) to those that are now technology enhanced. And we'd better. Given the choice of having Socrates or Bill Gates as a teacher, I know whom I would choose.

Increasingly the teachers and librarians who can survive and thrive in schools ever more permeated by technology will need to view themselves as "co-learners" in many learning experiences. Remember that "life-long learning" applies to us as well as the kids.

Technology Dinosaurs

September 2005

My dad never bought an answering machine—nor would he use mine when he reached it. When I teased him about this strange aversion, he would grumble, "When I want to talk to a machine, I'll go to the garage and visit with my lawn mower."

"What a dinosaur," I thought.

So now it's a surprise to look in the mirror and see another technology dinosaur looking back—me. A short list of the technologies to which I am now as adverse as my dad was to the answering machine includes:

- **Instant messaging/Chat.** IM has all the limitations of e-mail and none of the freedom to respond as time permits. I've used chat as a "guest" expert in online classes and find that I suffer from either premature or delayed articulation. Wherever the conversation is, I'm somewhere else.

- **Digital music players.** Music is fine in its place, but so is silence. Don't get me started on "podcasting." If I want news, I'll listen to NPR.

- **Cell phones.** OK, I admit I own one. It has 30 minutes a month call time and rides around in the pickup. I pride myself that I have made those around me so confident of their problem solving abilities that they need not contact me during meetings, while on vacation, or during a movie at the local bijou. And forget text messaging—do you how many times you have to press a number on the keypad to get the right letter?

- **Blogs.** The popularity of these shared "diaries" astounds me. When publicly commenting on professional matters, I find it challenging to find enough to say in a column a few times a year. I am far too slow a thinker to be "profound" on a daily basis. And why, for heaven's sake, would anyone want to read my musings on anything to do with my personal life, which ricochets from boring to embarrassing?

Perhaps what all these technologies have in common is that they are invasive. They simply cut into the time I would rather spend doing other things like reading books and journals, enjoying a quiet walk, concentrating on a task, or taking a nap. Perhaps being a dinosaur isn't a bad analogy. I'm a rather slow-witted creature who needs undistracted information processing time to make sense of the world. And all around me are these new young critters for whom information "now" is not quite soon enough.

Dad was a crop duster and using an answering machine never had much impact on his work. The farmers whose fields he sprayed didn't like getting an answering machine any better than he did—and the corn borers certainly could not have cared less. But as an educator, the decisions I make, especially related to information technologies, do matter. And even if I personally don't embrace blogging or text messaging, I need to have an understanding of both the technologies and my students who do.

A book I would highly recommend is *Educating the Net Generation* (Oblinger and Oblinger 2005). Sorry fellow diplodoci, the file of the complete book is only available for free downloading. If you've time for nothing else, read at least the first couple of chapters that describe the learning styles and preferences of the "Millennials" or "Net Gens" we are teaching today. The authors have synthesized many of the findings of researchers who look at how young folks are using technology and how that impacts their learning styles.

Understanding, accepting, and respecting the differences between most of us who are of the Boomer generation and our current students is important. We know this generation values visual media, individualization, collaboration, socialization, and experiential learning. They appreciate the human element of education, but want information access 24/7.

How does this respect translate into library and technology services? The Net Genners will appreciate graphic novels, increased reference materials online accessible from anywhere, and a good library Web site. They want physical libraries that encourage positive social interactions and collaborative learning. We need to encourage and co-teach constructivist lessons with our classroom teachers that allow kids to discover, rather than be simply told, information and conclusions.

I don't think it is unrealistic for us as professionals to begin using some of the popular technology tools to provide library services. How about a library blog related to the latest books and resources? Can your students contact you with questions via e-mail? Does your library offer wireless network access?

The Millennials have another nickname as well—the "Next Greatest Generation." Our young people are different from us in many and often confusing ways, but they are also motivated, academically oriented, and socially conscious. Let's go at least halfway in meeting their needs by using their tools.

Evolve!

Note: OK, so I may have been a little hasty in my evaluation of blogs and blogging.

Letter from the Flat World Library Corporation

March 2006

A few years ago, Linda, the Left Overshoe Middle School librarian, read Thomas Friedman's book *The World Is Flat.* She felt sorry for the legal researchers, medical technicians, and technology support personnel whose jobs were being outsourced to countries like India and China.

When Robert, the high school librarian, learned that a local business had closed its library and contracted its research to a private research firm, he thought it made good business sense.

Louise noticed an increasingly larger percent of her elementary budget was going to electronic resources, most of which were "packages" tied to her state's standards. Her teachers didn't seem to need as much help finding support materials for their units. She was glad to have the extra time.

All the librarians in the Left Overshoe schools encouraged their students to use a 24/7 electronic reference service because it worked so well with the district's one-to-one computer to student laptop initiative.

But Linda, Robert, and Louise met frantically one afternoon after school at the local pub to discuss a photocopy of a letter each of them received, along with a note from the superintendent. It read:

FLAT WORLD LIBRARY CORPORATION

March 15

Superintendent Dennis Hookworm
Left Overshoe Public Schools
Left Overshoe, Minnesota 56034

Dear Superintendent Hookworm:

We at the Flat World Library Corporation (FWLC) can offer you a complete library program at a *very* attractive price.

For considerably less than you currently pay for your K-12 library program, we can provide a full range of library resources AND library services—all on line.

For only pennies a day per student, FWLC will:

1. Provide a full range of reading materials (periodicals, picture books, fiction, and nonfiction titles), videos, and reference sources that are tailored to your state standards, your district's curriculum, and your digital textbook series. These resources are being constantly updated, and are available, of course, in a wide range of flexible ranges to support your differentiated instruction efforts. You can specify the level of community tolerance for issues ranging from abortion to gay rights to evolution from "university community" to "small town Kansas."

2. Provide ready reference services, student research help, readers' advisory service, and curricular planning advice through our real-time connections (video, chat, or e-mail) to our experts in Bangalore, India. These highly qualified MLS certified professionals will be available 24/7 to both your staff and students from school *or* home. (Do you get 24/7 service from your current library staff?)

3. Allow teachers to submit student work for comment and assessment. Our staff will give each project a consistent grade, check for plagiarism, and provide a report for each child that teachers can share with parents about the research and technology skill strengths and weaknesses of every individual student. We can even help your teachers design assignments and assessments, so they are free to lecture.

Just think of the advantages:

- No musty books from the 1950s cluttering your library shelves. No more lost or missing books.

- No library facilities. Turn that old library space into those badly needed special education classrooms.

- No more pesky librarians who want more money for materials, support staff, and staff development. Our highly skilled Indian librarians are happy to have their $5 per hour jobs!

- A single, semi-competent technician in your district can maintain your entire library program.

- You can justify your district's expensive 1:1 computer/student initiative.

- No more contentious book or curriculum "challenges."

Please read the attached study (scientifically based and conducted by FWLC's very own research department) that empirically demonstrates that this product can dramatically improve student performance where it counts—on high stakes tests. (FWLC has been approved by for Federal Title and grant funding—unlike traditional library materials and librarians.)

Act today!

Coming soon—special pricing for regional and statewide purchases.

Sincerely,

Bill Baudrate, CEO

Flat World Library Corporation
300 Gates Drive
Greenmond WA
1-800-NO-BOOKS

The penciled note at the bottom from the superintendent read simply: "Why should I *not* buy this product?"

Librarians 2.0

April 2006

The Web is a'changing, in case you haven't noticed. Web sites are out. Blogs are in. Posting articles is out. Collaborative writing using wikis is in. Reading the newspapers online is out. Reading personalized RSS feeds is in. The *Encyclopedia Britannica* is out. Wikipedia is in.

This is a change being described as a move from Web 1.0 to Web 2.0. Much of this change is due to new Web sites and software that greatly simplify posting one's writings (or photos or audio recordings) to places where they can be seen by the rest of the world. As a result, the Internet user has access to the observations, opinions, and advice of people who would not traditionally be considered "experts." And an exchange of ideas is not only permitted but encouraged.

Tools like RSS feeds are moving the information experience from "mass media" (few producers of information communicating with a large number of consumers) to "personal media" (many producers of information communicating with a more individualized group of consumers).

The implications are profound, and if we as librarians are to remain "information experts," we'd better master this new media. Let's take just three Web 2.0 applications you need to know about and think a bit about their implications.

Blogs. Kids have been "blogging" for years using social networking sites to share their thoughts with friends (and strangers.) But adults are catching on. Technocrati, a Web site that tracks blogs, reports there are about 77 million blogs as of 2008 with a new one being added every second. From their humble beginnings as political rants and personal displays of teen angst, blogs are becoming mainstream communication tools used by schools, businesses, and, gulp, even adults. Pioneering teachers are using them to facilitate classroom discussions.

Wikis. These online tools allow writings to be edited collaboratively. Post something and invite the world to change it—hopefully for the better. Wikipedia, a collaboratively written encyclopedia, is the premier example of this technology, but schools are using wiki software both in classrooms and in staff development efforts.

RSS feeds. Blogs, wikis, news services, and other Web sites that regularly update content can be subscribed to using their RSS feeds. Aggregators organize and monitor these feeds. A quick glimpse at a single Web site shows when something new has appeared in these Web 2.0 tools.

So what might be some of the implications for Librarian 2.0 whose patrons are Web 2.0 users?

New communication opportunities for schools and libraries. Check out Frances Harris's "Gargoyles Loose in the Library" blog. Harris uses this popular tool to communicate with her high school students about new resources, library activities, and even some personal adventures. (Gee, our librarian is a human being!) How do we use these tools, already popular with students, to strengthen our programs?

New evaluation skills. The popularity of Wikipedia has forced librarians and teachers to ask some hard questions about the definition of an "authoritative" source. Who is more credible? A magazine article or soldier's blog who is writing from the front? A professor who writes a textbook or front-line practitioners?

New safety concerns. The very ease of posting information where anyone can find and read it may compromise student (or adult) privacy. Pew Internet and American Life Project's *Teen Content Creators and Consumers* (Lenhart and Madden 2005) report finds that 57 percent of teens can be considered "content creators." What measures are we responsible adults taking to ensure students are taking their privacy seriously?

Loss of an exposure to a diversity of ideas. RSS feeds have made reading only the writings of those whose beliefs are similar to our own very easy. Even if readers only scan the newspaper, they will be exposed to a variety of stories. How do we as educators help students consider multiple viewpoints and broaden their interests?

New professional growth opportunities for librarians. An informed professional cannot responsibly wait until a technology, an issue, or a philosophy makes it into a mainstream print publication. Every librarian, even if not a blogger, can and should contribute to the dialog on professional blogs. How can we guide students in the use of something we ourselves have not experienced?

David Weinberger asserted in an National Educational Computing Conference (NECC) keynote address that information should not be considered a static entity, but an ongoing conversation. The Web 2.0 is your access into that conversation.

My Next Library Catalog Needs . . .

February 2008

Our library automation system sales representative is always after me to upgrade our current circ/cat system to the latest and greatest version. Sure, our libraries have been using this one for quite a while, but I just can't get excited about the current update. It just isn't a revolutionary leap in function and features.

I want to wait for at least some of these features in our next major circ/cat system upgrade:

1. **Federated searching of our own holdings—print and electronic.** With a single simple search engine, our students and staff should be able to search *everything* in our libraries—think of it as Google for everything that Google doesn't search. My student researchers could compile a list of potential resources ranging from magazine articles to book chapters to encyclopedia entries—high-quality materials that have been professionally edited. Making such information as easily found and accessed as the junk that too often pops up in a Google search would be sweet.

2. **Concordance searching.** Google's "Book Search" and Amazon's "Search Inside the Book" allow users to search by term or phrase the entire texts of books. Why should my catalog not allow internal searching of books in my local collection? As I remember, scanning an entire book for the Book Search project costs Google about three dollars. For my unique titles, spending a couple bucks to make them accessible is a reasonable investment.

3. **User-defined tags.** The ability to add personal descriptors of items stored on Web sites like Flickr have made the Dewey Decimal System and Sears subject headings look rigid and antique. Students and staff should be able to define materials in the library in ways that have personal meaning to them. (Similar to *Harry Potter.* Jane recommends. Good for Mr. Smith's physical science class rocks and minerals unit.)

4. **User reviews, readers' advisory service, and online book discussions.** Even the most dedicated librarian can read and recommend a finite number of titles. Online sites like Shelfari "make it easy to see what your friends are reading, what others with similar tastes have enjoyed, and even get and give book recommendations." Amazon, of course, encourages reader reviews and makes recommendations for future reading based on an individual's past reading history. As Jacquie Henry suggests in her Wanderings blog, should her catalog be asking:

How about. . . . . . . "people who checked out this book, also checked out these other books. . . ."

How about. . . . "let us know what you think about this book."

How about. . . . . "join a chat/discussion group about this book."

5. **Ready-made citations.** Why not have the functionality of the NoodleTools bibliography composer built into your catalog? For those of us who never really got the hang of APA or MLA or whatever, it would be a blessing. It would take away some of the suspicion that academic research is best left to the most anal-retentive of society.

6. **User networking tools.** Customizable social network spaces like Ning and tools like wikis make online collaboration on projects made simple. When offered in house as a part of the library automation system or in a stand-alone application, such tools allow students to continue working and learning 24/7.

7. **Seamless interface with student information system to facilitate data mining.** Allow searching and sorting by NCLB "student groups" to track circulation. Can I demonstrate that my efforts to get more books in the hands of our ELL students have been successful?

8. **No cost to our libraries.** Perhaps we need to reexamine the financial model for how we pay for our library automation systems. Most of us are accustomed to Web resources that come at no direct expense to us. They may be supported by advertisements or by premium subscribers wanting more features. While this is not my favorite idea, being able to apply more of my library budget to purchasing materials rather than on automation software or annual maintenance is appealing.

We are indeed starting to see some of these features in current library systems. But are they coming fast enough? Our students are accustomed to having these tools and features on Web sites they already use. If their library resources are to remain relevant to them, shouldn't we offer these things as well? How do we make authoritative sources as easy to find and access as the questionable materials? And how to we appeal to the social natures of our Net-Gen patrons and help develop their collaborative skills?

We as school librarians need to be more vocal, more demanding of our circ/cat providers. Now—before we become completely irrelevant to our students.

Reflection

> If you don't like change, you're going to like irrelevance even less.
>
> —U.S. Army Chief of Staff (ret.) General Eric Shinseki

I have been using Amazon's Kindle e-book reader for about a year at the time of this writing. While it by no means the perfect reading device, it is sufficiently functional that the technology does not stand between me and the reading experience in any meaningful way. And the benefits—light weight, long battery life, huge storage capacity, searching abilities, and easy access to new books—overcome any of its limitations.

The only thing standing in the way of this device or one like it from replacing all print books is the current inability for publishers to figure out how to provide their titles to users without also making them available to "unauthorized" users. The fate of the music recording industry is making them nervous and cautious.

But this paralysis is surely temporary and will buy libraries only a very little time to consider how to adjust to digital texts read on silicon books.

I've used the column "Letter from the Flat World Library Corporation" that appears in this chapter in workshops for the past few years to willfully scare the hell out of librarians. I am not sure how well it worked on the participants, but re-reading it always scares *me*.

Skepticism about technology is wise—many times the future takes longer to get here than we thought. But so is fear. Realizing that as digital information systems mature to become affordable, transparent, and ubiquitous, libraries will need to change or simply fade away is an awful vision.

Is there a real battle between print and electronic services? While initially frightening to many of us—that our beloved books and libraries would be replaced by terminals and computer labs—a gratifying number of librarians have grown to appreciate the access to digital information sources. In fact, we've come to love them for how empowering they can be both for our students and for ourselves.

Technological change asks us to closely examine our role in schools. What do libraries provide that the Internet cannot? What will our role be in managing digital resources? How can we be proactive rather than reactive as the world becomes increasingly digital? On reflection, I see these questions as not only of utmost importance now, but of even greater importance in the future. If you haven't noticed, the pace of technological change is not slowing down. Quite the opposite.

Let's get this one right, fellow librarians. I have grandchildren who deserve good school libraries.

CHAPTER 5

On Technology in Education

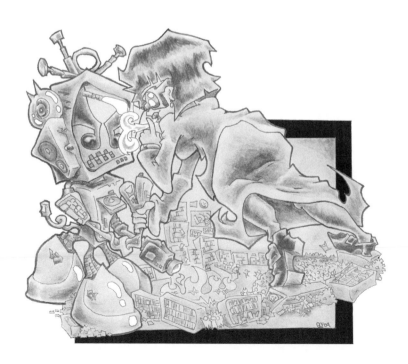

WIIFM?

December 1996

Before I can convince you to accept an idea, try a new procedure, or support a cause, I have to help you answer the WIIFM question: *What's In It For Me?* This old psychological chestnut is worth dragging out and examining every once in a while by educators interested creating any type of change in their schools.

The WIIFM approach is really at the heart of most effective persuasive efforts:

- The telephone company uses it: We'll give you better rates and services.

- The YMCA uses it: We'll give you a longer life and the health to do more things.

- Politicians, the clergy, and educators all use it: You'll be better off after the election, in the next life, after graduation.

WIIFM is a powerful tool for those of us who would like to see education transformed into a process that is more effective, works for more children, and has a more positive effect on society, using information technologies as the transformational catalyst. But we need to be careful. Too often the WIIFM question when asked by teachers is answered by technologists with a quick, "Technology will make your life easier." Just invest about 200 to 300 hours in training and practice, and your electronic grade book will calculate your grades for you!

As my son would say—Big Whoop.

There are plenty of good reasons teachers need to put some serious "butt-time" into learning new technologies, but efficiency is not necessarily one of them. Instead WIIFM should be answered and proven with arguments like:

1. The skilled use of technology will give a more professional look to your communications, help you create more effective self-made teaching materials, and allow you to better organize your resources.

2. Technologies, especially online communications, can open more opportunities for professional development and collegial contact. Educational materials like study guides, lesson plans, and assessment

tools are easily and inexpensively obtained via the Internet or other online sources.

3. The more technologies you have, the greater variety you can inject into the school day, and the more opportunities you have to be creative. Kids aren't the only ones who get bored in school.

The problem with these answers to the WIIFM question is that their veracity is difficult to substantiate by quick and easy measurement. Increasingly, many people value only the things they can measure. It takes a leap of faith on the part of teachers to accept that investing time to learn to effectively use technology will not necessarily make them more efficient, but it will make them more effective.

Appreciate those teachers who are willing to make that leap. Most skills that are worth having require work to master. Learning requires genuine effort. New knowledge often makes us uncomfortable or even frightened. Work, effort, and discomfort—I'll accept them all, so long as I know WIIFM.

One excellent thing makes the job of the technology advocate easier. Teachers respond not just to a WIIFM approach. In fact, the WIIFMS argument is often far more persuasive: *What's In It For My Students?* We are still the most altruistic profession on the face of the earth, regardless of any political rhetoric to the contrary.

Here are just a few ways research and experience has shown technology (and especially information technologies used in conjunction with resource-based teaching and learning) can answer the WIIFMS question:

1. increased learning, more efficient learning, higher level learning

2. increased motivation and sustained interest

3. higher percentage of students reached and involved (at both the high and low ends of the academic achievement curve)

4. opportunities to learn whole-life technology skills that can strengthen student's natural abilities and talents

Notice that not one these benefits includes, "Technology will make learning easier or more fun"? Technology can make learning possible in many cases, but not necessarily enjoyable. The pleasure of learning with technology is derived from the same sensations the pleasure of all learning comes: feeling that I am smart and capable of growth; recognizing that I have additional tools to use on real problems; and discovering that I have new lenses with which to view life.

An honest statement of WIIFMS should be a part of every budget proposal, every staff development activity, and every technology plan. And teachers aren't the only ones who need to learn WIIFM(S). So do parents, community members, administrators, and, yes, even our students.

A Cautionary Column

May 1997

The final result is that technology aids our thoughts and civilized lives, but it also provides a mind-set that artificially elevates some aspects of life and ignores others, not based upon their real importance but rather by the arbitrary condition of whether they can be measured scientifically and objectively by today's tools.

—Donald Norman

I have spent an unhealthy amount of time this weekend designing an online electronic survey. After this database is finished and administered, I am hoping that the resulting data will tell me a great deal about how much our teachers use technology, how well they use it, how accessible it is to them, and how important they feel it is to their jobs. This data then can help our technology leadership team make some informed decisions.

Informed decisions—what a concept!

This database will be but a single flake in the blizzard of data within which our school operates. To help manage and use all the things we know about kids, parents, curriculum, assessment, finance, transportation, and so forth, we are creating an information strategic plan. The need for it has come for several reasons:

1. Proliferation of unconnected databases. In the data storm we have lots of individual scoopers and scrapers. (Can you tell this has been a long winter in Minnesota from the analogies?) How much of these information sources sound familiar to you? Individualize Education Plans, Student Management Systems, Report Cards/Progress Reports, Gradebooks, Resource/Facility Bookings, Library Catalogs, Curriculum Management Databases, Attendance Records, Personnel Files, and Health Profiles. If it currently exists as a paper form in our district, you can bet it will soon be "digitized." The problem is that little of this is connected. A single child's name may be entered in as many as a dozen separate databases, and then reentered when he advances a grade or moves to a new school. What percent of those databases have the child's name spelled the same way? We are all scooping without a coordinated effort.

2. Increased speed of the networks. Networks are making it practical for a single, high capacity, speed file server to be used by all buildings in the district. One shared database will be able to share some or all of its information with smaller databases in the district. When a single flake of information about a child changes, it will change in all databases.

3. New accountability requirements of the community and state.
Accountability seems to have been *the* only vocabulary word our state legislature. It's probably time. Schools' requests for new or continued funding will be contingent on more measurable data, and that means comprehensive, accurate record keeping. Both the government and parents want schools to do a better job of keeping track of how much kids are learning. This information is neutral and will be used in lots of ways—some of them controversial: for tracking students, for comparing schools, or even for discovering and meeting individual's needs. Like it or not, you as an educator will be asked to measure and record more and more.

Now I have long been an advocate of using good data to justify budgets, communicate program efficacy, and just plain determine if what one does is making a difference. I am really good at counting how many books are checked out, how many teachers attended my in-service, or how many computers are in the district. (Sometime I do have to take off my socks when I run out of fingers.) It behooves us all to find ways to answer the question: is my library/technology program making a difference? As Tom Peters writes: "What gets measured, gets done." I believe it.

Yet we can't afford to lose sight of some of the "immeasurable" effects of schooling, library programs, and technology.

- How do you measure the learning atmosphere in a building or room? Is there excitement, creativity, and joy evident in your program? What kind of feeling does a person get when entering your school or room? Is there an eye gleam meter or a smile-o-scope and creativity scoring bubble sheets?

- How can you differentiate between children who are intrinsically motivated and those who work only for a reward? How do you tell decision makers that it may well be those who love to learn and work rather than those who do well on basic skills scores that will contribute most to society? Where are the "flow" rubrics and the concentration scales?

- How do you measure the degree to which students feel they are cared for, valued, and respected? And how do you quantify the degree to which students in turn care for, value, and respect other in the school? Do we need a caring account code or a good deed database?

Take some time away from school and technology each summer. Connect with your family and friends. Read a book just for fun. Learn a skill that has no use except for the joy of doing it. Reconfirm what you know deep inside about children, what you really love about education, and why you entered the profession. And when you get back to school next fall, remind the decision makers of Mr. Norman's caution in the opening quote: that there are things of value that cannot be measured no matter how good the technology.

Examining the Enchantment of Technology

September 1997

I don't know if there are any empirical studies to back me up, but kids do behave better while they are using technology. Librarians and teachers agree: the more computers are used in the library or classroom, the less discipline is a problem.

From what I've observed, it doesn't really seem to make much difference what type of activity students seem to be doing with the technology. Drill and practice, keyboarding, word processing, searching the Internet, or working on a slide show all seem to precipitate this often sought but too seldom found occurrence: our captive audience engaged in a learning activity that gives more satisfaction than the attention gained through misbehavior.

There may be a number of reasons for this:

Novelty. The "Gee-Whiz" factor is high with technology. That newest simulation, graphics program, or animated Web site often grabs our attention with new bells and whistles. For many of children coming from low-tech homes, any computer itself can be a new experience.

What novelty doesn't explain is why so many children continue to use certain programs for extended lengths of time, why not all software has staying power, or why children who have grown up surrounded with technology remain enthralled. In fact, the children who have had the most experience with technology are often are the ones most absorbed by it. That "geek" syndrome.

Entertainment. A good deal of software written for education is deliberately designed to have entertainment value. So much so, the entertainment elements sometimes overshadow the educational purpose. I am as amused as the next person by bright colors, catchy tunes, and cute cartoon characters of many children's software program. For at least five minutes anyway.

Overall, entertainment hasn't really succeeded very well as an educational tool. That's mostly due to the fact that we are generally passive while being entertained, and the images and sounds do not change each time we use the computer program or view the video. As I have discovered by watching *Toy Story* with my son at least 10 times, even the most clever and creative amusements become less so with repetition. Just ask my wife about my jokes.

Involvement. Activities then need to change in some way each time we engage in them in to stay compelling. In the book *Flow,* psychologist Mihaly Csikszentmihalyi (1990) asserts that there are common characteristics of involving (flow) tasks. Among those are that a person's skills are being used at a level that is challenging, but not frustrating; that the participant is receiving continuous feedback; and that the tasks have defined goals or standards of completion.

Computer games, including drill and practice programs, certainly have Csikszentmihalyi's flow elements: continuous feedback, a variety of levels, and a defined criteria for advancement to the next level. (And the "reward" interestingly enough is a more difficult assignment.) The problem with arcade-style software is that one rarely gets to practice skills that go beyond kinetic memory or factual recall. You have to love those little *Number Munchers,* but students will never be asked to apply the learned math skill to a real-life situation no matter proficient they become at the program.

Thinking Required. I will advance a final, radical notion. Kids like technology, not because it makes learning easier, but because it makes schooling more challenging. As I recently discovered when shadowing a student for a full school day, it is *boring* when you are only asked to just listen and repeat. It's not hard to see how the "blank slate" analogy came into being—just look in kids' faces who are being regarded as such.

There has never been a desktop publication created, a database designed, a videotape shot, a spreadsheet constructed, or a question answered through electronic research without a good deal of actual thinking going into it. In fact with most productivity software, users get a double dose of thinking: they get to design both the content and the container of the content. Student fascination with technology is not with the technology itself. What technology users find compelling is the reflection of their own growing ideas brought forth by the technology. The best computer programs extract and enhance our creativity. They clarify and organize our thoughts. They color and diagram our plans. Whether in the form of a director's video camera, a musician's keyboard, or a writer's word processor, technology at its best makes our uniqueness visible to the world.

Wouldn't it be surprising if we one day discovered that the most difficult tasks we ask our students to complete, those that really require originality, creativity, and reflection, are the ones they like the best?

The School of Hard Knocks

March 1998

So Ole visits his college advisor and admits that while he is interested in the sciences, he has a difficult time keeping them straight. "Yust, do vat I do, Ole," his advisor suggests. "Remember dat if vat you are studying is green, it's biology. If vat you are studying smells bad, it's chemistry. And if vat you are studying doesn't verk, it's technology."

Most of us at one time or another have had technology fail while we were trying to use it to teach. A first class meeting of a college course I taught could be used as a textbook example of just how many things could go very wrong in a very short period of time. The interactive television connection could not be established but still made an annoying, unstoppable noise; the telephone in the classroom interrupted every few minutes; and my computerized slide presentation decided to develop seizures. Even the tried-and-true copy machine had skipped some of the pages of the syllabus.

Oh, the class I was teaching was "Introduction to Technology in Education."

Of course the students enjoyed my discomfort immensely and regarded with deep skepticism my promise that the class was to be a model for how technology can be integrated into the learning environment. I went home that night ready to start applying for jobs that did not include the use of anything that needed to be plugged in or turned on. Unfortunately, organic farmer, busboy, and school superintendent were the only alternative paths that came to mind.

So it was in this curmudgeonly frame of mind that I developed the following list of lessons from the school of hard technology knocks. Feel free to add your own.

Technology makes good communications better and poor communications worse. Someone once said that the copy machines duplicate human errors perfectly. A poor speaker amplified does not make things better for his audience. Poor spellers using a word processor can no longer hide spelling uncertainties with sloppy handwriting. Bad organization is exacerbated with a computerized slide show. Sounds and animations cannot make up for a lack of content in a multimedia presentation.

If you want a teacher to use technology, it had better be reliable. It's really hard to get a teacher to use a new technology again when it doesn't work the first time. As the proverb says so well, "Once bitten, twice shy." The lesson for the technology coordinator or librarian is to check, test, and try everything thoroughly before putting it in a teacher's hands, especially if that teacher has the slightest reluctance to using technology. And don't do it the hour before it is to be used, but a day or preferably a week before. I am continually amazed at how many times I have seen a technology demonstration by a salesperson bomb. Why would I buy a product when the "expert" can't make his own stuff work? Would I go to a surgeon who cut himself shaving that morning?

Don't expect appreciation for improved technology. People only notice when it isn't there or it doesn't work. Last year I got at least three calls a week complaining about the speed of our computer network. During the summer we increased the bandwidth more than tenfold. It's now well into the school year and do you think I've head one word of how nice the fast network is? Of course not. I estimate it takes less than a month before an effective technology introduced into a classroom is simply taken as a given by its users. "Huh, haven't we always had telephones and computers on our desks and projectors in our ceilings?"

People don't come and get information. You have to send it to them. Few people will pull up a school's Web page to check for announcements on a regular basis. Paper notes sent to the recipient work, electronic mailing lists are effective, and RSS technologies show promise. But depending on a Web page to provide timely news can't be relied upon. That's why the newspaper is delivered to your door.

For some people the risk of using technology is so great, that they won't use it unless it is impossible to do their job with out it. No matter how many teachers you get to read their e-mail, file attendance electronically, or use the electronic catalog to check for materials, there will be a small percentage who simply refuse. They will invent ingenious work-arounds to keep from touching stuff. They will train students, rely on other teachers, or go without. These folks as a rule are neither stupid nor belligerent, and I at am a loss to explain why they are so resistant to the digital way of doing things. Perhaps they had bad experiences with small appliances as very young children.

Technology can be a great excuse. "I know I sent it to you. The e-mail must have lost it." Technology is the new way of saying, "the dog ate my homework." In my experience the networks, the e-mail, the fax machine, the voice mail, and the electronic library catalog work with 100 percent reliability—or they do not work at all. It's easy to tell. But people being people, they will look every place but at themselves when things go wrong.

Pardon my grumpiness. I'm sure I'll be in a far better mood soon. Provided I find the lost file I was just working on. Darn computer must have eaten it.

Faith-Based Computing

September 2001

If you think you can do a thing or think you can't do a thing, you're right.

—Henry Ford

Knock on wood, but I have been pretty darned lucky with the personal computers I have owned and used. For some years I've not experienced any of the catastrophic hard drive crashes, regular freezes, or major data losses about which one commonly hears. And my computers get hard use. I use the same personally owned laptop for both my workstation at school as well as for my private business and personal work. It goes home with me every night and travels with me in airplanes and in the toolbox of my pickup to conferences and even on the occasional vacation.

Sure, I make backups. Yes, I run a systems diagnostic tool once in a blue moon. Of course, I keep my virus protection program up-to-date. And especially, I don't let my teenage son within 15 feet of this computer.

Some technologies, like some people, are just plain high maintenance. But many computer users take these precautions, but still experience trouble. So why am I so "lucky"?

The techies and I have discussed at length what seems to be a districtwide phenomenon we call "Faith-Based Computing." The basic tenet of this theory is that the more positive the user's attitude toward technology, the better the technology works for that user. Simple as that.

So how do these supposedly non-sentient boxes of plastic, glass, and metal pick up on our human vibes? Maybe there is something operating on a quantum level as electricity passes through computer chips and networks much as it passes through our human nervous system. As silly as it sounds, we are careful not to say negative things about any computer when another networked computer is in the room. They listen and talk to each other, you know. Remember Hal? We are careful to make sure in offices with two computers that both of them get attention so neither gets jealous. We've even discussed the theory that computers, like cats, are often happier when there are two together, or at least when there is a digital clock or framed picture of the user nearby.

I know. This is beginning to sound like a *Weekly World News* article or conspiracy babble, but there is definitely a connection between user attitude and user success in most endeavors. We've had the concept of "self-fulfilling prophecy" in education for years. Why should technology use be any different?

Most schools survey their teachers occasionally to find out how skilled they are in computer use. It's an effective means of determining where staff development opportunities are needed. "Yup, looks like quite a few folks could use an advanced Web page creation class," we may determine.

But here's the thing, we need to measure not just skills, but attitudes as well. If it seems our teachers are making only minimal progress toward using and integrating technology, it may well be that negative attitudes are getting in the way. (And probably making the machinery obstreperous as well.) Teacher reactions to statements like the ones below can give a glimpse of where there might be attitude problems in your school:

One a scale of 1 to 4, with 1 being strongly disagree and 4 being strongly agree, please respond to these statements:

1. Using technology makes me a more effective teacher.

2. Technology helps me organize my work.

3. I find the use of technology to be motivating to students.

4. I am comfortable learning about and using technology.

5. I would like to integrate more technology into my work.

6. I would like to integrate more technology into my classroom units.

7. The building administration encourages the use of technology.

8. The district administration encourages the use of technology.

9. I feel comfortable helping others in the school with technology.

10. I feel comfortable asking for help with technology from others.

11. The district provides me a variety of opportunities to learn technology skills.

12. I take personal time to learn and practice technology skills.

If one finds that there are definitely negative attitudes toward technology use by a significant number of teachers in your school, here are few things that can improve technology morale. Stress the WIIFM (What's In It For Me) reasons for computer use. Give the end user (teacher) a voice in deciding equipment platforms, software adopted, and timelines for implementation. Take a hard look at your in-service times to make sure they are as convenient as possible for teachers. Adjust the attitude of the technology support staff. As all of us help teachers with computer hardware and use problems, are we doing our best in making sure they are respected for the intelligent, loveable people they really are?

It's important to remember that teacher attitudes don't just affect technology, but students as well. As staff developers, we have an obligation to help maintain not just a skilled staff, but also a happy one.

Now please excuse me while I dust my computer's keyboard with that soft cloth she likes so much. Got to keep her purring.

Did You Hear the One About . . . ?

September 2002

Users are expected to use Internet access through the district system to further educational and personal goals consistent with the mission of the school district and school policies.

—from the Mankato Area Public School Board
Policy 524: Internet Acceptable Use

OK, I'll admit it. I *like* the fact that e-mail is a terrific source of jokes. I receive them, read them, and pass them on. Sometimes it's on school time and on my school e-mail account. And I have a tough time feeling very guilty about it, even though it might be difficult to reconcile this use of the Internet with our school's acceptable use policy. What does my reading "The Top 10 Signs You've Joined a Cheap HMO" have to do with "the mission of the school district"?

It's part of my job to help ensure good technology use by both staff and students in our district. But I more often than not turn a blind eye to personal use unless it is egregiously inappropriate. We do strictly enforce the use or distribution of pornography or any image that co-workers might regard as creating a hostile work environment. We don't tolerate harassment or entrepreneurship conducted using school networks by anyone.

But I recognize that teachers e-mail their kids in college, explore possible vacation destinations, or place an online order to Land's End now and again. I recognize that these folks are professionals and that lessons will be planned and homework graded whether at school during a prep time or at the kitchen table after supper. It's the nature of professionals. And professionals need to be accorded professional respect.

We've even set up two distinct districtwide mailing lists. The first list to which everyone must be subscribed is for official school business. But the second mailing list is used for the sorts of things you might find on the bulletin board in a teachers' lounge: personal items for sale, announcements of upcoming arts events, news items of possible interest, and suggestions of Web sites that might be of non-educational interest to teachers and staff. Subscription to this list is voluntary.

Why not take the hard line approach to enforcing a school acceptable use policy? It has everything to do with climate. I can't help but think that unless it affects job performance, personal Internet use makes the school a more enjoyable place to work. Teachers have enough stress in their lives. A little humor lessens the stress, makes for a happier teacher, and this is a good thing. After all, would you want your child with an *unhappy* teacher?

As librarians and technologists, I think we need to lighten up a little in regard to what students are doing with the Internet in our libraries and classrooms as well. The Internet has vast resources that are not directly related to the curriculum but are of high interest to students at all grade levels. Information about sports, fashion, movies, games, celebrities, and music in bright and exciting formats abounds.

The use of the Internet for class work must be given priority, but computer terminals should never sit empty. And there are some good reasons to allow students personal use of the Internet:

It gives kids a chance to practice skills. After all that's why we have "recreational" reading materials in our libraries. Do we really subscribe to *Hot Rod* or *Seventeen* because they're used for research? If we want kids who can do an effective Internet search, read fluently, and love to learn, does it make much difference if they are learning by finding and reading Web pages on the Civil War or Civil War games?

It gives weight to the penalty of having Internet access taken away. The penalty for misuse of the Internet is often a suspension of Internet use privileges. As a student, if I were restricted to only school work uses of the Internet and had my Internet rights revoked, I'd pretty much say, "So what?" and wonder what I had to do to get my textbooks taken away as well. But if I'm accustomed to using the Internet each morning before school to check on how my favorite sports team was faring, the loss of Internet access as a consequence of misbehavior would be far more serious.

It makes the library a place kids want to be. Many of our students love the library for the simple reason that it is often the only place that allows them to read books of personal interest, work on projects that are meaningful, and explore interests that fall outside the curriculum in an atmosphere of relative freedom. Kids need a place like that and we should provide it—even at the Internet terminals.

We can't throw out the rules. But we can and should recognize that schools are comprised of human beings. And we need to do everything we can to make school a human-friendly place for both staff and students.

Oh, and the number one sign you've joined a cheap HMO?—*The tongue depressors taste faintly of Fudgesicles.*

Reflection

Putt's Law: Technology is dominated by two types of people: those who understand what they do not manage, and those who manage what they do not understand.

Back when God's dog was still a puppy, the AASL standards included "instructional consultant" as one of the librarian's three major roles. When I first read this, I thought it sounded pretty pretentious. Hey, I'm just another teacher. Who am I that others should be "consulting" *me* about how they teach? I wrote it off as just one of those loopy things thrown into standards by the library school professor on the writing committee.

That was until technology integration started to become the Holy Grail for many principals who were under pressure from the central office to justify some enormous expenditure. The "ready, shoot, aim" method of getting computers in schools happened more than we would like to admit. And in some places it is still the operating principle.

The technicians and teachers who "got" technology early on came by it through some innate ability, some mystical sixth sense. And people for whom something comes easily don't always make the best teachers since often operations seem *so* obvious to them. Plus the technophiles on the teaching staff were busy—teaching.

As a librarian, I never saw myself as a technologist, but simply as a technology user. In fact the use of even the word processor was a struggle for me. And some days it still is. But I also could see the power of such devices and felt all students should learn to use the devilish things. And the only way all students would learn them well was if all teachers recognized and used them themselves.

So I became an "instructional consultant" (heaven knows I never used that term in the teachers' lounge) on the applied use of technology. And my successes came not from my natural abilities, but my lack of them. I usually needed to create some sort of analogy trying what I was doing on the computer to something in the real world. Uh, OK, sending an e-mail is sort of like sending a letter. It needs an address and a message and serves the same purpose. I also realized that one needed to be careful and also figure out when the analogy broke down. Hmmmm, if I put a period at the end of an address in a letter, it will still get there. If I put one at the end of an e-mail address, it won't. Tricky.

My personal need for simple instructions, good analogies, and a true conviction that what I was learning was important to students when figuring out technologies translated into making me pretty fair at teaching other teachers how to use it as well.

And here all this time you thought I was some sort of techno-god. Sorry to disappoint.

The other reason that this was a good fit was because as a librarian, I was among the few staff members with much discretionary time during the school day. I was plenty busy in my traditional role of librarian, but seemed to be able to squeeze in a few hours each week to learn something new and develop ways for others to learn it as well. I had all that time I once spent filing catalog cards after we automated. School librarian and technology integration specialist were a combination that worked—and gave me added value to my Grail-seeking principal.

Other factors that make librarians the best possible choice for taking on this job include our willingness to be lifelong co-learners; our understanding that technology is not the answer to every problem; our collaborative spirits; our own curriculum that is infused with technology skills; and our concern for the ethical and safe use of information and technology. And that we are very, very charming.

On reflection, the columns in this section were written to support the librarian who, like me, also serves as a technology specialist in her school. I now wish all our professional standards included our role as "instructional consultant."

CHAPTER 6

On Managing Good

Six Ways to Beat the Study Hall Syndrome

November 1995

A librarian new to the profession recently asked me, "How does one keep a library from becoming a study hall, recreation area, or dumping ground for students?"

Ah, this was a battle I also seemed to fight over and over in my years as a building librarian. In every school and at all grade levels, some teachers and administrators often saw the library as a "holding area." I believe it is an endemic problem.

To get to the heart of the problem, it helps to understand that education is only one of three tasks with which society has given its schools. The other two—child confinement and child socialization—seem to be particularly apparent in the less structured areas of the school: the hallways, lunchrooms, and libraries. Of these areas where students have freedom of movement, discretionary time, and a choice of activities, the library is the only one that has an academic mission as well. While we need to acknowledge that libraries must share the school's obligation to contain children and must honor children's need to socialize, librarians can and should bring the academic mission to the fore.

So how can we do this?

Schedule plenty of meaningful activities. If the library is being used by whole classes doing research or other kinds of study, the physical plant will not accommodate large numbers of non-directed students. The teachers of the classes using the library will help support and enforce a climate of purposeful activity.

Add technology to your area. Tables full of idle children tend to cause problems; students at computer terminals, whether involved in writing, searching, drawing, or even playing, rarely do. While I have never felt it was the school's job to entertain children, I certainly believe it is our duty to involve them. And few things involve this generation of kids like interactive media. Fill your libraries with technology, not empty tables.

Share your space with other big people. The more adults in your library, the more likely you are to have a productive area. Make a space for an adult-run study skills center, for the talented and gifted program, for parent volunteers, or for other academic support programs that need a home. The old idea of the library being a hushed room behind closed doors is passé. Work is not always a quiet activity; learning is usually accompanied by terrific sounds: laughs, questions, instructions, sharing, surprises.

Have few rules. All my libraries, K-12, operated under three simple rules for all patrons. To stay in the library one needed to:

- be doing something productive
- be doing it in a way that allowed others to be productive
- be respectful of others' persons and property.

That's it!

If I were to run a library again, I might just adopt the one rule that governs the Glen Urquhart School in Massachusetts: "No student has the right to interfere with the learning of another student or the purpose of an activity." The key to simple rules is working with children and teachers on common understandings and applications of them. For example, is reading a magazine being productive? Is napping? Is cartooning? Is playing a computer game? Consistent enforcement of such rules is challenging, but good for kids who as adults will be asked to apply guidelines to their behaviors, rather than only adhere to set rules.

Provide alternate activities. Have things for students to do who do not seem to have schoolwork. Provide books, newspapers, and magazines for personal interest reading. "Reading practice" materials, I like to call them. Design activities like reference scavenger hunts, puzzle centers, or individual viewing of videos. Save a few tasks for the physically restless students: putting up bulletin boards, reshelving materials, dusting, shelf reading, collection mapping, equipment maintenance, magazine check-in, or newspaper bundling.

Change the school climate. Teachers and the principal of your school need to share your vision of the library as a place for work, for learning, for productivity. If they don't, your job will be nigh on impossible. You can change the views of your staff by sharing successes your program has afforded students. Educate teachers about current library philosophies and your goals. Serve on your site-based management team to make good school policies and rules—especially those that apply to your library. Work to change teaching strategies so that the resources the library provides are essential to the educational process. Help your school find other options for the containment and socialization functions of the school—restructured days without study halls, student commons, open gymnasiums, or intelligent schedules.

Folks, we all work in the real world. I have had plenty of study halls in my libraries when the principal simply couldn't find another room large enough. Plenty of my patrons have been the kids a teacher or study hall monitor simply couldn't stand for another minute. Some kids have come to my library for every reason under the sun but to study. Did I ever create a perfect learning environment—an intellectual gymnasium? Nope.

But I know that my libraries were places kids found interesting, safe, non-threatening, rich in interesting materials and activities—not to mention sort of helpful when they needed information. As one of favorite classroom "ejects" occasionally reminded me, "Mr. Johnson, the library is my home away from home." High praise.

Giving and Taking

October 1996

In light of the current political climate about taxes, those of us in public education should revisit David Lewis's "Eight Truths" about budgeting (Lewis 1991). His first Truth is just as applicable now as it was when published years ago: "It is a zero sum game." When talking about public library budgets, he explained: "There is no more money . . . The important truth is that those who provide the cash . . . will not give the library any more. They can't because they don't have it." Schools, as well, seem to have reached a level of funding that the public is unlikely to substantially increase. Does this mean no additional funds for your library or technology program?

Not necessarily. Mr. Lewis suggests a way that middle managers (like librarians) can get more money for their programs: "You can take it away from somebody else. If you believe in what you are doing, you have an obligation to try this." Gulp.

This puts an awful lot of us outside our comfort zone. Aren't we really "givers" of resources, skills, information, time, and effort? Fighting for an adequate budget, especially if it means butting heads with co-workers like department chairs, band directors, coaches, custodians, or union reps, certainly feels like being a "taker." Want to make an enemy? Threaten the funding of a program that is owned by another educator.

But look carefully at the second part of Mr. Lewis's statement—"If you believe in what you are doing, you have an obligation to try . . ." Folks, we better all believe deep in our hearts what we are doing is in the very best interest of our students and community, that spending what is necessary for an effective library and technology program is better than buying new textbooks or violins or smaller class sizes.

So here's the deal. You really need two psychological weapons when fighting to make your program a budget priority: a thick skin and a deep-felt mission. Without them, you'll get eaten alive; with them, you can accomplish anything.

Strong feelings and fearlessness are of course greatly helped by a strong rationale for your budget. Today's budgeting committees really need to be asking questions like:

- What programs teach the skills that will be vital to tomorrow's citizens?

- What programs, skills, and attributes does your community believe are important?

- How many teachers and students will benefit from a particular spending decision?

- How might a budget decision affect the school's climate?

- Is there research to support the effectiveness of a program or specific spending decision?

- How much budgeting is being done out of respect for sentiment or tradition?

As librarians, we need to do our homework. Our budgets must be specific, goal driven, and assessable. They must be both accurate and easy to understand. (Learn how to use a spreadsheet—you'll never regret it.) And I hope our budgets are supported by research and sound reasoning.

One powerful way to convince others you should be given additional funding is to remind them how successful you have been with your past budgets. Remind them about how many people your program serves and how much of the curriculum depends on it. Get others on the staff to support your budget or items in your budget.

Don't just deal in numbers. Let folks know how individuals, both teacher and student, have been helped by your program. The one common denominator that all effective salespeople have is the ability to tell a good story—to personalize the facts. Hey, and who can tell stories better than we can? "You should have seen the kids lined up before school opened to get into the library to use the new computers. You all know how Johnny Smith never gets excited about anything in school. If you'd have seen him find the NASA Web site, you wouldn't have recognized him."

Finally a last quote from Mr. Lewis, something to think about when you have a few quiet moments: "It is unacceptable for others in your organization to misuse resources that could be better put to use by you." Thanks, Mr. Lewis, for helping us see that we need to learn to be effective "takers" if we want to be good "givers."

Advisory Advice

October 1997

No, this month's column is not sponsored by the Department of Redundancy Department. I am advising you to form an advisory committee if you don't already have one.

Such a group can be a great help for the librarian at either the building or the district level. My advisory committees have given me terrific ideas, huge challenges, and timely warnings over the years. The first group I formed was just a few teachers and a couple of parents from the high school where I was the librarian. For a little wine and cheese, these wise folks would leave their families and far more interesting activities to come to my house and talk about libraries and computers and how adolescents learn best. We hammered out an articulated vision of what a library program should do. They helped me set my professional goals, and then listened when I reported my trials and triumphs. It was the best deal I ever made. My advisory committees have become larger and more formal since that time, but they still serve very much the same purpose: to help me make better decisions.

After having been served by and served on a number of these committees, I offer some advisory advice:

Keep your group small. Any committee much larger than a dozen is difficult to get together and difficult to bring to consensus. If you need a much larger representation, keep your full meetings few and do most of your work in subcommittees.

Work for a wide representation of stakeholders who serve limited terms. My current committee is comprised of teachers, students, board members, and administrators, of course. But parents, business people, a multi-type library representative, and post-secondary educators also serve. Our computer coordinator and network manager are permanent members. We don't have a set selection process for membership, but no one serves for more than three years. Remember when selecting your members, that communication is a two-way street. What your representatives learn at your meetings will be taken back and shared with that person's colleagues. Great public relations.

Have few, but important, meetings. Advisory committees only need to meet three or four times a year. A fall meeting is a good time to establish working subcommittees and refine the year's goals. One or two meetings to work on budget or policy issues in the winter and a final spring meeting to review the year's work and set objectives for the coming school year are enough. Setting our meeting dates for the year at our first meeting makes them a priority for many members. Take attendance, and include who is there in your minutes.

There are several guides to running effective meetings on the market. Buy one and read it. Your committee will thank you, and it beats trying to remember Roberts Rules of Order.

Send out good agendas and write clear, concise minutes that are quickly distributed. If members see agenda items that they think are important (how the budget is to be divided up this year, for example), they'll be more likely to attend. All my advisory group members use e-mail, and we rarely send hard copies of anything through the mail. I e-mail myself a copy of all agendas and minutes for easy filing and retrieval.

Finally, give your group well-defined responsibilities. A committee should not be making your professional decisions for you, but it should have the power to shape the direction of the library/technology program. And well it should, since these folks, as well as you, will be held responsible for the program's weaknesses as well as its strengths. My advisory committee works on:

- long range planning and goals and my department's yearly objectives
- budgets
- policy making
- program assessments

And that's about all the work we can do.

Ours can be a professionally lonely profession. In all but the largest schools, there is rarely more than a single librarian or tech coordinator. We are outnumbered by kindergarten teachers, custodians, coaches, special education aides, and administrators. An advisory committee is one way of giving ownership of the library program to a body of stakeholders in the building. If the goals, the budget, the assessments, the long range plan are known to be important to more than just a single person, when they are presented to decision makers, they will carry more weight. And if your advisory group includes parents, community members, and students, it will be seen as a very important body indeed.

No Principal Left Behind

March 2003

All administrators can learn.

"If only my principal could hear what you just said!" is the wistful comment I hear time and again after giving a keynote presentation at conferences. Indeed, a lack of understanding by administrators about what good school library programs can be and should do is widely regarded as detrimental to the profession.

Professor Gary Hartzell often reminds us that there is little mention of school library programs in administrative preparation programs, and that when libraries are mentioned, it is because they may be the source of problems such as book challenges or copyright problems. There is also a pretty good chance that your principal may not have had the opportunity to work with a great librarian before you came along.

That leaves it up to you, the individual school librarian, to help inform and educate your principal about good school libraries and the positive impact they have on students. Below are some tips gathered from conversations with effective school librarians about what works:

1. **Use a variety of formal reporting efforts.** We should all be sending out a written or e-mailed quarterly principal's report and a monthly faculty bulletin. These should be upbeat, useful, and short. Every newsletter that goes to parents needs a library column. Think about including digital photos of happy library-using kids. If your state library association has "advocacy tools"—handouts, videos, checklists, and so forth—use them whenever you get the chance. Take advantage of regional events that may be planned in your area. For example, many New York BOCES agencies hold an annual

breakfast for school librarians and their administrators that feature an informative program. State library conferences often have special events just for administrators.

2. **Remember that administrators HATE surprises.** Your principal does not like to be surprised by either good *or* bad news about your library delivered by someone other than you. As a true administrator, I like knowing of bad things in advance so I can figure out someone else to blame. I like knowing about good things in advance so I can figure out how to take the credit. Your principal should *never* learn about something happening in your library from a teacher, a student, or, especially, a parent.

3. **You need to view yourself as your principal's ally.** You need your principal's support, of course, for funding, program building, and helping influence other staff members. Did you ever think that your principal needs you too? As cheerleader and co-conspirator for change efforts. As staff development resource for new programs. As an educator who can positively affect the learning environment of the whole school. As a researcher for best practices information. How exactly does your principal rely on you?

4. **Know your principal's goals and interests.** Can you rattle off right now the three or four things your boss considers important in your school? Test scores? Climate? Meaningful technology use? Figure out where your goals and your principal's goals overlap. That's not sucking up—that's being politic.

5. **Try to speak on behalf of a group, not just for yourself.** Principals really listen to the comments of parents and community members. (Ever notice how it only takes three concerned citizens at a school board meeting to change a policy?) If you can submit the library goals and objectives, the budget, or program initiatives on behalf of an advisory group that includes parents and community members, you are more likely to be taken seriously.

6. **Be seen outside the library.** If your principal sees you on committees, attending school events, and even in the teacher's lounge, not only can you chat informally about library matters, but you send a powerful non-verbal message as well: I am full member of the school staff.

7. **It's OK to disagree with your principal.** You may think that some ideas of your principal may not be in the best interests of your students or staff. If that's the case, you have an ethical duty to give your reasons to your principal. But this is important: do so in private. Always voice your support in public; always voice your differences in private.

8. **Do *not* whine.** You are not going to want to hear this, but there is a little riddle that goes around administrative circles: What is the difference between a puppy and a teacher? The puppy stops whining when you let it in the door. What exactly is whining and how does it differ from constructive communication efforts? Robert Moran (1994) says it best: "Never go to your boss with a problem without a solution. You are paid to think, not to whine." I know it feels good to just let it all out sometimes about things that really can't be changed. But listening to that sort of venting is what your spouse, your mom, or your cat is there for.

9. **Advocate for kids, not for libraries.** Advocating for libraries sounds, and usually is, self-serving. When you talk to your principal whether proposing a plan, asking for funds, telling what's happening in the library, volunteering to serve on a committee, agreeing to help with a task, or suggesting a solution to a problem, the underlying reason behind it should always be: "It's a change that will be good for our students." Period.

10. **Remember that you have a professional obligation to be a leader as well as a follower.** Our communication efforts can and should not just inform, but persuade others, guide the directions of our organization, and improve our effectiveness. If we don't create the positive changes in our schools that improve kids lives, just who the heck will?

Good communications are never accidental. A well-informed principal can be a truly supportive leader, but it is up to each of us in the profession to communicate, to inform, and to teach "up" as well as "down."

Let's leave no principal behind in creating better learning opportunities with better libraries.

Top 10 Things Baby Teachers Should Know about School Libraries

April 2003

Dear First-Year Teacher,

Welcome to school. Is it ever nice to see your fresh, smiling face! I hope some of your eagerness and enthusiasm rubs off on the rest of us who have been here awhile. A couple of us still yearn for the days of the one-room school.

I am the school librarian. Or media specialist, if you prefer. I answer to both. I recognize that your teacher preparation may not have given you much information about with working with me or using our library's resources effectively. There is also a good chance that the school library you used during your own school days was different from our program here.

To help get things off on a positive spin, here are a few things I'd like you to know about the library, our program, and me that can help us form a great partnership . . .

1. **The librarian doesn't own the library.** You and your students do. You can recommend materials and have a voice in library policy making. Volunteer to become a member of our school's library advisory committee.

2. **The library should be considered an "intellectual gymnasium."** It's not a student lounge, study hall, or baby-sitting service. The students in the library, including the ones you send, should have a reason for being there. Whether for academic purposes or personal use, students should be in the library because they need the library's resources, not just because they need to be *somewhere.*

3. **The best resource in the library is the librarian.** I can help you plan a project, solve a technology problem, find professional research, give insight into an ethical problem, or answer a reference question. And if I can't do it, I will help you find someone who can. I can help find and inter-library loan materials you need that are not in the school library itself. Helping others gives me a huge sense of satisfaction so please never hesitate to ask me.

4. **Planning is a good thing.** Advanced planning with me will greatly increase you and your students' chances for success with projects that require information resources. A *well-planned* research unit or technology project will greatly decrease frustrations for everyone involved. With my experience, I can let you know what strategies work and don't work.

5. **Recognize that the library provides access to both print and electronic information.** I can determine which format best suits yours and your students' needs. Students do not always realize that print resources are better for many purposes. It breaks my heart to watch a student spend a frustrating hour trying to find the answer to a question on the Internet that could have been answered with a print resource in minutes.

6. **The librarian can be helpful in evaluating the information found on the Internet.** One of the greatest challenges of using the

Internet is determining whether the facts and opinions found there are credible. I have the training and tools to do just that. And it is my mission to teach students effective evaluation skills as well.

7. **The librarian can help create assessments for your students' projects.** The findings of research projects presented in electronic form, conclusions drawn from primary resources, and research that calls for higher-level thinking to be demonstrated, all call for good authentic assessment tools rather than a simple gut-reaction comments or an objective test. I can help you find examples of these sorts of tools as well as help you create and administer them yourself. Let's work together to make your students' learning experiences as meaningful as possible.

8. **The librarian can be your technology support center.** I'm no technical guru, but can help you and your students with technology applications. Need to use a scanner or digital camera? I can show you how. Need to create a multi-media presentation? Let me give you a quick lesson. Looking for effective ways to search the Web? Ask me. I'm not a technician, but I can help locate that kind of help for you as well.

9. **The library can help your students' performance on standardized reading tests.** Research has proven that children become more adept at reading by extensively practicing reading at or just below grade level. The library contains a wide range of material in print format that students can use to improve reading skills. And I can help match just the right book or magazine with just the right reader. If you need a booktalk for your class or help with a student struggling to find something of interest, just say so.

10. **The librarian will be your partner when trying new things.** It's been said that some teachers during their career teach one year, 30 times. Can you imagine how long those 30 years must have seemed? If you need somebody to share the glory or the shame of a new unit, activity, or methodology, I'm the one.

I hope your career will be exciting and gratifying. You'll be influencing the lives of hundreds if not thousands of kids in incredibility positive ways.

The subtitle of my professional standards document is *Building Partnerships for Learning*. I have truly taken that concept to heart. I am here to help you and your students do things you can't do alone.

Again, welcome,

Your Librarian

A Valentine

February 2004

Sandy. She was my first. She was older . . . and experienced. I was young and innocent and a little frightened. I wanted nothing more than to be good at what I did. Sandy was patient, caring and oh-so wise. She taught me the "little things" I could do, but also helped me see what I did within the larger picture.

There have been others since Sandy. A Bonnie, a Donna, a couple of Janes. Each in her own way very special. But it is Sandy who helped make me the man I am today.

Sandy, this Valentine's for you.

A quick quiz: From whom did you learn the most about running a library?

a. A college professor

b. A fellow professional librarian

c. Your first library paraprofessional

For many of us the answer is c. It has been my good fortune to have had the experience of working with amazing clerks, secretaries, and library paraprofessionals throughout my career. These unsung heroes of the library world are underpaid, are underappreciated, and are among the most important people in the school.

Too often I have forgotten that the paraprofessional is really the "face of the library." These are the folks our staff and students often encounter first when they come into our space. Paras are whom they deal with on a regular basis. And whether that face is smiling or frowning makes a huge impact on the library's climate.

In my experience, students rarely differentiate between the library professional and paraprofessional. My youngest library users often called me "Mr. Palardy" or Bonnie, my aide, "Mrs. Johnson" simply assuming Mrs. Palardy and I were married as well as being co-workers. I am sure it embarrassed Bonnie profoundly.

The most accurate description of how most paraprofessionals are treated is "benign neglect." Sure, we are friendly. We bring a flower on "Secretaries' Day." We smile at the pictures of their children or grand-children when they make the rounds. But how much do we really address the "professional" part of "paraprofessional"?

For all the Sandys and Bonnies out there, let's resolve to:

1. **Get them out of the building.** Paras need and appreciate staff development opportunities just as much as we professionals. Learning about new trends in librarianship, about new student educational resources, about new customer service skills, and about using new technologies are needed staff development opportunities for paras. We all feel better about ourselves when we feel more competent about we do. State library conferences often have a strand for paraprofessionals. Watch for state conferences especially for paraprofessionals.

2. **Support their formal training goals.** The path taken by some of our best professional librarians started with the librarian as a parent volunteer, then as a library para, and finally as a professional librarian. If some of your support staff show an interest in getting a library degree, encourage them. We need all the quality people in our field we can get.

3. **Value their contribution to the team.** Build on the recognition that you and your para's skills are complimentary. I am *not* a detail person, and the best clerical and technical people with whom I work are. The simple acknowledgement that all skills used by the library's staff are important is essential.

4. **Include them in planning and policy-making.** One of my favorite stories tells of a janitor at NASA in the late 1960s. When asked what his job was, he replied, "To help put a man on the moon." Support staff members should know not just their jobs, but how those jobs are critical to the mission of the library program and school. One way to build this understanding is by making sure they have a voice in visioning, planning, budgeting, and policy-making.

5. **Encourage their creativity.** If your para wants to read the kindergarteners a story, what's the problem? If she has dynamic idea for a display or reading promotion, why not encourage her? Clerical tasks can be stultifyingly dull. The chance for your para to do something creative, exciting, and different not only helps prevent job burnout, but can be of genuine value to your program

6. **Run interference for them.** It's not the para's job to take heat from disgruntled teachers or parents. The best professionals protect and defend their support staff. You pick on my para and you'll answer to *me*!

Finally, we need to harness all our interpersonal skills when working with all staff, including our support staff. Darlene Severance (n.d.) has a wonderful list of "do's" and "don't's" when working with paraprofessionals. It's worth reading a couple times.

> So, dear Sandy, accept this small token of my appreciation. You taught me above all that behind every successful professional librarian is a competent paraprofessional. You'll be special to me always.

Whose Voices Are Most Powerful?

November 2005

Not every story has a happy ending and I'm afraid this is one of them. But even sad tales can be instructive.

I received a call early one summer from a librarian in a small, near-by district; let's call it Left Overshoe Independent Schools. She asked if I, as a representative of the state library association, would speak to Left Overshoe's school board arguing against her district's budget reduction plan since it included cutting half a librarian position. I agreed to do this and developed a short multimedia presentation with persuasive research findings, heart-warming anecdotes, and lots of photos of happy, library-usin' students. On that lovely June evening of the board meeting, I was well prepared and felt optimistic as I hopped in the pickup truck and drove south.

The Left Overshoe board meeting was an interesting experience. The superintendent, who did not seem terribly pleased to see me, insisted that I not use the PowerPoint presentation. "The board can't handle it," he said. Only four of the six board members were there even though (or maybe because) budget reductions were on the agenda. The district's two librarians whose positions were not threatened were there in solidarity. The rest of our small gathering included the head of maintenance and a couple principals.

Anyway, I spoke for about 10 minutes about the impact of good school library programs on student achievement, their impact on life-long learning, and their positive influence on school climate. The board members paid attention, laughed in the right places, expressed appreciation that I was willing to attend the meeting, related how much they all personally supported books and libraries, and bemoaned how difficult times were financially for the district. And went right ahead and voted to cut the library position.

Rather than being angry, I left the meeting feeling rather sorry for these citizen volunteers for the hard choices they had to make. Along with the library position cut, a school bus route was eliminated; a two-hour-a-day mentally handicapped man who did lunchroom duties was fired; the head custodian's pay was reduced from $12 to $10 an hour; a vacant math position in the high school was not filled; and once again much-needed roof maintenance was delayed. When one of the board members asked why there were no "administrative cuts," the principals reminded him that they had already absorbed the duties of the Title I coordinator, curriculum director, and standards coordinator without any additional compensation. Judging by the quality of his suit, the super-intendent was not overpaid. None of the cuts were made without a good deal of thoughtful discussion and few votes were unanimous.

But it was one comment by a board member that really hit me hard and is why I am telling this story. He asked, "Why, if this library cut is going to have such a serious impact on our students, have I not re-ceived a single phone call from a teacher, parent, or student objecting to it?" I thought it was an instructive question. Just a few teacher or parent voices (maybe only one) in support of the library position would have been far more persuasive than I could ever have hoped to be at that meeting.

There is an old literary term called *deus ex machina,* literally "god from the machine." It's a dramatic device used when the plot of a play became so hopelessly complicated with the hero facing such an impossible odds that the only way the playwright could create a happy ending was to literally use a piece of stage equipment to fly a "god" on to the stage who would magically set everything aright. The dragon was slain, the heroine brought back to life, and the hero reconciled with this family.

If your district may be contemplating library staffing cuts this coming year, let your state school library association know about the cuts and do so early. It may well already have a "crisis response" in place that will help you fight the cuts. But don't rely on it for a *deus ex machina* ending.

Today, start lining up the local teachers and parents who would be willing to testify to your board about the good things in your program and how cuts would be harmful to students. While the expert from more than 25 miles away will be listened to politely and the research acknowledged, the people board members have to live with on a daily basis will always have far more credibility and power.

And if you can't find people who will speak against library cuts? Perhaps a critical assessment of your program is needed.

Voices must be raised when library programs are threatened by budget cuts. They just can't all be ours.

Common Sense Economy

January 2005

Share everything.

—Robert Fulgham in *All I Really Need to Know I Learned in Kindergarten*

In times of tight funding, decision makers in schools ironically forget that libraries were invented because information resources are often scarce. Clay tablets, papyrus scrolls, vellum manuscripts, and even the printed book have all been rare, expensive to create, and unaffordable by many individuals. Humans, being the social, clever, and trusting creatures that we are, figured out that information could be held in a single location and then systematically shared among a group. Libraries were born.

So why today do many educators seem to think of libraries only in terms of costs rather than savings? Perhaps we need to remind them that libraries help maximize the use of resources by:

Creating a common pool of shared materials. There is not much argument among educators today that reading ability improves when kids read more, and that readily available reading materials help make that happen. Book fairs, "guided" reading kits, and classroom libraries are all designed to put more books into the hands of more kids. And "that's a good thing."

When things get tight financially, however, doesn't it make sense to go back into a sharing mode? Classroom collections can and should be drawn from strong school library collections. Besides economy, the collections can be rotated to keep reading materials fresh. The real beauty of a common collection is that materials purchased for individual units get double or triple duty: in gifted programs, ELL programs, and by students pursuing individual interests. I just despise the thought of a wonderful resource that is tightly locked in a teacher's cabinet for 90 percent of the year.

As Fulgham in the opening quote suggests, we should share. It is not only the moral thing to do, but a smart financial move as well.

It's cheaper to buy a book for the library and share, than it is to buy one for each classroom. Duh!

Tracking materials. It plays to the stereotype, but yes, part of the job description of the librarian is to make sure the "stuff" is accounted for. We do stamp/engrave/sticker, catalog, circulate, and inventory common school property. We remind students (and teachers) that materials should be returned in a timely manner, especially when there is a high demand for those materials.

When materials go directly into the classroom, not only are they are far less likely to be an asset for the entire school, but they may not be available for long even for students in individual classrooms. Teachers rarely have as good a system for tracking who has what material out. When teachers change classrooms, buildings, or districts, the materials often go with them. Even "classroom" materials, should be inventoried and tracked by the school library, whether they are specially purchased classroom libraries, AV resources, or equipment. When teachers retire, resign, or transfer, part of the exit procedure should be a clearance from the library.

Selecting the most useful materials. Spending $1,000 on new materials, of which only 20 percent are used, is no better than having spent $200. Because of training, access to reviews, knowledge of the whole school curriculum, and just plain old experience in knowing what kids like, the librarian is very, very good at picking materials that will really be used.

Promoting and teaching the use of materials. Like many states, Minnesota provides some common, commercial online resources to all schools. But according to the director who oversees these databases, some schools use them heavily, others very little. All schools in the state are now "wired," share a common set of academic standards, and have children that are all above average. What causes the variation in how much these state-provided resources are used?

While I don't have quantitative evidence, I'd be willing to bet real money that the schools that use the databases have a librarian that is aware they are available, teaches others how to use them, and promotes their use.

No book, magazine, database, video, Web page, or computer program jumps off the shelf into a potential user's face and says, "Here I am, here's how to use me, and here's why you should use me." The librarian is the voice of those resources. Educational dollars are wasted when materials remain "untouched by human hands." And even sadder than the waste of money is the loss of learning opportunities these resources could provide.

A few years ago, those of us representing libraries at a state legislative day wore buttons and carried balloons that carried Anne Herbert's fine words: "Libraries will get you through times of no money better than money will get you through times of no libraries." Perhaps we should wear those buttons all the time and put a balloon on every superintendent's and school board member's desk.

The Power of Parents

November 2006

In many communities the reality is that today's parents have as many choices of schools as they do fast food restaurants. And choice gives parents power. Administrators understand that parents, not children, are the education system's true customers, and that customers can and do vote with their feet. If parents' expectations are not met, they will pull their children and all those lovely state aid dollars that come with them out of the displeasing school and into another educational venue. As a result, administrators are listening more carefully to parents now than they ever have in the past.

Wouldn't it be nice if parents would share this power with librarians, adding their voices in support of strong library programs? Actually they will and are delighted to do so, but not without some conscious effort on the part of the librarian. Here are a few ways I've seen clever librarians harness the power of parents:

Use parent volunteers whenever possible. We often look at parent volunteers as a source of "free" labor, but these workers, when treated with respect, develop a sense of ownership in the library and library program. Cultivate your volunteer program by giving parents not just routine tasks to do like reshelving materials, but challenging, meaningful jobs like conducting story times, creating displays, and working-one-on-one with students. Do your volunteers have any special interests or talents that can be harnessed? We've had amazing parent artists paint murals on our library walls.

Include parent representation on library advisory committees. An active library advisory committee *must* include parent representatives.

Administrators read plans, budgets, and policies coming from groups with parent representatives carefully.

Work closely with parent-teacher organizations. Savvy librarians attend PTO/PTA meetings, participate in their events, and help with fund-raisers. We need to help such organizations meet their goals as well as getting help from them to meet ours. While many librarians know to go to the PTO for funds, we sometimes forget that the members of these groups are very influential among all parents and in the community. If you're going to suck up, this is the place to do it. The best gift that PTOs can give libraries is not money, but support and influence—especially in times of budget crisis.

Grab the attention of parents during open houses and parent-teacher conferences. Special displays, events, or even the presence of a coffee pot will get parents in the door of the library during times parents are in the building. Is a sign-up sheet listing a variety of ways they might get more involved in the library as volunteers available? Is there a bulletin board or a multimedia presentation showing the cool things students are doing in the library clearly visible? Do you have brochures about your program that can be distributed?

Allow parents to check out materials for use with their children at home. Make it clear that parents are welcome to use the resources of the library themselves. Not every community has a good children's collection at its public library and many parents appreciate books that can be taken home to share with their children. I've always made sure parents know that they can use computers or other equipment outside of school hours as well.

Take the "library program" to the parents and community. "If only people would visit and *see* what actually goes on in the library, they would understand its value!" is a sentiment I hear often. A short video showcasing the library and students actively using it can have the same impact. It's portable and available anytime there is the chance to meet with parents or community groups. Invest the time in making one.

Establish a formal and regular means of home/school communication. A more passive form of "participation" is just making sure all parents know what positive activities, events, and resources are a part of the library program. *Every* school newsletter going home to parents needs a library page illustrated with digital photos of happy, library-using kids that educates parents about what is happening in your program.

If a school board cuts a sport, reduces a special education service, or increases a class size, parents turn out in droves. Parents should show up to object when library cuts are proposed as well. But they won't do it unless we cultivate the relationship.

Starting off on the Right Foot

May 2009

Dear Great Brain,

I need to write up my goals for the year and give them to my principal. I have a few general ideas such as collaborating with teachers as much as possible, becoming a good resource for them, teaching students to use the databases, starting a lunch time book club, and decorating the library with student art. If you could send me any other ideas that seem reasonable for a first year in high school it would be much appreciated . . . I love creative ideas.

Diane

Whether graduating from library school or beginning a job in a new building, newbies should give starting off on the right foot with students and staff a high priority. What's the old chestnut? "You never get a second chance to make a first impression."

While the tasks Diane lists above are important, they aren't particularly strategic. In other words, Diane is planning day-to-day activities. A big part of one's first year ought to be laying the foundation for growing and strengthening the program in future years as well. One should plan for both a happy and a *long* tenure in any new position.

My advice to all librarians beginning new jobs is based on *Johnson's Three Commandments of a Successful Library Program:*

1. Thou shall develop shared ownership of the library and all it contains.

2. Thou shall have written annual objectives tied directly to school and curricular goals and bend all thy efforts toward achieving them.

3. Thou shall take thy light out from under thy damn bushel and share with others all the wonders thou dost perform.

Say, that's pretty good. What do you think the job of biblical prophet pays nowadays?

Based on these commandments, I'd recommend these first year goals for any library program:

Establish a library advisory committee comprised of teachers, parents, and students. The library programs that are the most effective, the most appreciated, and the most secure are those in which everyone in the learning community has a stake. An official committee is the best way of creating that ownership and shared responsibility for success. Oh, get on your building's improvement committee/leadership team ASAP as well. Shared governance goes both ways.

Establish yourself and program as ally to your principal. If you know and can help solve your principal's principle problems, you will establish yourself as an important member of her team. All the principals I know are being asked to make some serious changes in educational practices. If you can help midwife new methods of instruction and programs, you will be gold. If you are seen as irrelevant, you will be gone.

Work with your committee and your principal to establish collaboratively created goals and a realistic budget. You may wish to conduct a library survey and do a collection evaluation to give direction to these goals. These do not need to be long and arduous, but the information should help you determine the past program's strengths and weaknesses. Conducting a staff survey also shows you are genuinely interested in helping teachers meet *their* needs. A good collection evaluation will help form the basis of writing a budget that is specific, goal-oriented, and realistic.

Quickly establish a formal communication plan. Think of the four main groups with whom it is vital to communicate: your students, your staff, your principal, and your parents. Identify current communication tools—newsletters, Web pages, e-mail lists, display areas—and establish a library presence in all of them. Develop your own means of communicating with those you serve or whose support you need. Parents, especially, need to know how the services, resources and skills your program offers benefit their children. And all this needs to be done on a regular, repeated basis.

Start thinking about how you will demonstrate your program's impact on student achievement. Start collecting data your first day on the job. Circulation stats, of course, but also track how many lessons you teach, how many collaborative units you do, and how many individual requests you fulfill. Figure out early what numbers are most meaningful to your principal and teachers. You will need numbers one day and you might as well have the right ones.

By all means, newbies, develop those individual collaborative projects with teachers right away. But don't neglect a long-term, systematic approach to developing a program that has buy-in by the entire school and community. You need an entire learning culture that values and uses the library's program and resources, not just a few enthusiastic teachers. Being strategic means getting off on the right foot—in anticipation of a long, successful journey.

Oh, the e-mail was addressed to the collective "great brain" that is LM_NET, not me. But you already guessed that.

Reflection

> Management is doing things right; leadership is doing the right things.
>
> —Peter Drucker

> You can't do the right things unless you know how to do things right.
>
> —the Blue Skunk

I am getting a little tired of the emphasis on "leadership" in society and especially in education. For all the talk, all the theories, all the studies, and all the exhortations, this obsession is getting us nowhere—and good management may be suffering as a result.

Here are some deadly warning signs I've noticed lately . . .

- Has your local graduate school replaced its "administration and management" classes with "leadership" classes?
- Have your professional organization's standards become a "visionary" document instead a practical description of and guidelines for effective programs?
- Has your last administrator been hired based on his philosophy and not his track record of running schools well?

I will state right up front that I am a better manager than I am a "leader." On reflection, the workshops and writings of which I am most proud tend to be "management" rather than "leader" focused. Budgeting, tech planning, policy-making, skills integration, effective staff development, and program evaluation are among my favorites. It's pretty easy to sneer at sharing "how-I-done-it-good" stories rather than academic research or high-blown commentary. But those looking down their noses probably aren't the folks trying to make actual changes in a real library.

Let's face it—anybody can create a "vision" and cry loudly about all the things that are wrong and paint a utopian view that sounds pretty good. And it seems like almost everyone does. But what is usually lacking are any practical means of moving from Point A to Point B— especially within the parameters of working with real people, real budgets, and a real number of hours in a day. I would contend that true genius is in finding ways to make vision reality—working where the rubber hits the road.

I've been wondering a good deal about what seems to be a round of recent political, economic, and educational disasters—the Iraq War, the handling of Hurricane Katrina, the housing bubble, NCLB, the economic meltdown—and questioning whether it was a lack of leadership or piss-poor management that created (or exacerbated) the mess.

Lets see:

- removing an evil dictator and establishing a democracy in the Middle East—good vision, poor execution.

- helping the victims of a natural disaster—good vision, poor execution.

- increasing the number of people who own their own homes—good vision, poor execution.

- assuring that all children have reading and math skills—good vision, poor execution.

- instilling public confidence in our financial institutions—good vision, poor execution.

Where did we go wrong? Might it have been putting people in charge who couldn't organize a one-car parade? So-called leaders instead of excellent managers?

Pat a good manager on the back today. And strive to be one yourself.

CHAPTER 7

On Determining
Our Values

Mischief and Mayhem

December 1997

Ex abusu non arguitur in usum. (The abuse of a thing is no argument against its use.)

A very distraught high school teacher came to see me last week. It seems an anonymous someone had sent an e-mail message using Aaron's return address. The message wasn't very nice at all, and Aaron was insistent that the technology department (meaning me) find a way of keeping this from ever happening again. "A career could be ruined by such an incident," he fumed.

While I could certainly understand why he was upset, I don't believe I gave Aaron the answer he was looking for. No foolproof mechanical means of keeping people from sending e-mail under a borrowed or assumed name exists. Any e-mailer or Web browser allows a user change the return address. Anonymous mail services are easy to find. Digital signatures are still on the horizon.

Network management systems let us keep track of who was using what computer to do what when. But when an incident of suspected misuse occurs, who has the time to check the logs of every networked computer in the building? We can't even assume that the e-mail was sent from the school. It is as (or more) likely that the offending e-mail in Aaron's name was sent from a private home, the local university, or the techno-coffeeshop a few blocks away. Should we even automatically assume it was a student?

Sending an anonymous or misattributed e-mail is analogous to an obscene phone call or an unsigned note. Easier to do perhaps because there are no fingerprints, no voice, and no handwriting left in the ether. But trying to remember that similar things happened before there were computers and networks is sometimes hard to do. Electronic communication is still largely strange to most of us, and human beings tend to be wary of strangers.

Aaron is a good teacher. He's young and enthusiastic, and likes to use technology with his kids. His character and reputation will keep him from being seriously considered as the sender of the bad e-mail. My sense is that we may all have this happen to us sooner or later. We can only hope our reputation carries us as well.

Misuse of technology is not uncommon in schools. No matter how diligent teachers and administrators try to be, students will work around the new password, print 500 copies of Miss April to the office computer, wantonly trash files, or engage in electronic harassment. It is this generation's version of tipping outhouses, stealing watermelons, or putting the Volkswagen on the school roof. The problem is that we adults can't identify with the electronic havoc from which our students now seem to get so much delight, since we ourselves have not committed it and most likely don't understand how to do it.

It starts young too. Our middle school was having a bad time with its ceiling mounted televisions randomly turning on and off, switching channels, and gaining and losing volume. The sets worked in the shop, but back in the school building they acted up again. Until one day a teacher discovered a student with a special watch. It had a built in television remote. What a delightful sense of power that student must have felt for a few weeks!

Of course not all technology misuse is harmless. Electronic threats to the President have resulted in visits by the Secret Service to a number of schools. The potential for destroyed data is very real, as "crackers" gain a Robin Hood–like status with some students. An obscene message, regardless of its method of delivery, can be traumatizing, and the thought of a computer that controls a dam's floodgates being unofficially accessed is terrifying. Intentional or unintentional, the potential harm resulting in technological mayhem is quite real.

How can we as educators respond?

- If a student's use of technology violates a school rule, deal with it as you would any incident. The consequence of sending a harassing e-mail should be the same as the consequence of sending a harassing paper note. Searching a computer file should be treated no differently than searching a locker.

- Set up as few "challenges" to students who delight in getting around the system as possible. If a machine does not need a password, don't give it one. Rely on human control and observation rather than mechanical controls.

- Teach netiquette at the same time you teach technology skills. Allow student input into technology policy making and planning.

- Give students ownership of the system. One of our technicians deliberately seeks out the school's potential crackers and gives them responsibility for lab security. What's the expression—"It takes a thief . . ."?

- Don't take an incident any more seriously than it really is. If we are truly giving students choices, we have to accept the fact that some students are going to make bad ones. But learning and growth result.

It is human nature to test a system, cause mischief, and subvert authority. But humans also live by rules, act for the common good, and respect the rights of others. Good cybercitizens can be developed if we as adults don't blindly overreact.

Creating High Temptation Environments

September 2000

From: "Screwdisk" <sdisk@inferno.org>
To: "Wormwood" <wormie@terrafirma.edu>
Subject: Creating a high temptation environment
Date: Mon, September 18, 2000, 11:10:19 -0500
X-Mailer: Microsoft Outlook 8.5
Importance: Scorching

My dearest Wormwood:

Once again it is my unpleasant duty to report that your quota for new student souls lured to the "dark side of the force" (their argot, not mine) was *again* not met during the past school year. Agents consulting with districts similar to yours are consistently meeting and usually exceeding their goals. But I am sorely afraid that your performance has simply not been smokin'.

Since you were apparently sleeping during the last in-service, I will remind you of some of the ways the Internet can be used most elegantly to tempt young sinners to greater sin. Much of the Internet truly is a devil's playground. Hate groups, bomb-making instruction, views of sexual practices even we down here had not imagined, and access to a wide assortment of wildly deviant individuals are all online beckoning to troubled souls.

Unfortunately some schools (like yours!) have managed to keep access to these dark resources extraordinarily limited to their students. But here are some fiendish ways you, Wormwood, can help the schools in your circle create high temptation environments:

Install an Internet filter. Oh, the wonderful thing about these faulty programs is that they lull well-intentioned adults into thinking they are *preventing* access to our sites. (The irony makes my tail positively curl with delight!) Install and walk away—how simple. But as we both know, no filtering program totally blocks all "our" sites. New nasties are added each day and the URLs for old nasties often change. Some of our best sites have absolutely no textual indicators that can be picked up by even the most sophisticated algorithms. Plenty of sites devote themselves to teaching users how to defeat such blockers. Wormie, nothing helps our cause like a false sense of security.

Filters give us added bonuses too. We pick up a good number of children who have never been taught to be self-filtering as soon as they leave their "safe" school havens. Oh, and the blocking of sites deemed "controversial" helps prevent schools from creating informed decision makers. Happily we have the full support of many parents and politicians on this one. How would many of our legislators get voted in if they came from districts of thinking voters? Humans capable of independent thought and informed decision making? Scary enough to make these hairy old knees knock.

Make unsupervised computers available. In their rush to make sure all students have Internet access, well-meaning adults have put such access on *all* the computers in their schools, not just those easily monitored. Sad to say, humans are far less likely to do bad things when they know they are watched. Make sure that even computers not easily seen from a teacher or librarian's desk have Internet access.

Disregard security issues. Humans are such trusting souls—thank Beelzebub. They keep the same password (child's name, pet's name, phone number) from year to year, from application to application. Teachers even *give* their passwords to students. Secretaries willingly give passwords to complete strangers on the telephone if those individuals claim they are checking network security. Our more adept pupils can install hidden programs that record keystrokes, including those used to type in passwords. How delicious—it's like leaving the door to the candy store unlocked. Make sure there is no uniform school policy on mandatory password changes!

Make sure your district has no clear curricular uses for the Internet. Ahh, idle hands always were and always will be the devil's tool. Ever since Old Smoky coined the phrase "surf the Net," great numbers of young users under the dubious learning objective "learning to use the Internet" have been surfing into some quite hellish places. And the incredible thing is that they are, as the teacher would put it, *on task!* Take a class to the public library to research, let's say, countries, and little Johnny heads to the adult fiction section and opens Harold Robbins. The teacher can say, "Johnny, get back on task." Take a class to the public library to "surf the collection," and little Johnny rides a wave over to

Harold Robbins. Now the teacher can't say "Johnny, get back on task." He *is* on task—the task of exploring the library. Remember Screwdisk's Observation: nonguided technology use is even better than misguided technology use.

Forget appropriate use as a part of staff training. Be very careful about staff development in your schools, Wormie. A teacher or librarian wise in the ways of the Internet is a most dangerous opponent. Hell help us when adults finally figure out what kids are actually doing! Let's hope schools keep up the fine work in restricting teacher technology training to "How to Create a Web Page" and "PowerPoint Basics."

Ignorance leading to the blind observance of a particular belief has always been our greatest ally. This free will business has turned into a real double-tined pitchfork when young people are taught to do the *right* thing. Yet with diligence and just a little effort, ignorance is surprisingly easy maintain.

Fire up, Wormwood! Fire up! Follow these simple instructions and you'll meet your quota yet.

Insincerely,

Screwdisk

With apologies to C. S. Lewis

Freedom and Filters

February 2003

Like many school districts, ours was coerced into installing an Internet filter during the 2001 school year. We did this to comply with the Children's Internet Protection Act (CIPA) guidelines, and so remain eligible for E-Rate funds in our district.

So now after many years of vociferously and publicly advocating for filter-free Internet access for students, after convincing our school board and technology committee of the wisdom of unfiltered access, and after doing a darned fine job of teaching teachers and librarians why and how to supervise kids using the Internet, we ourselves are filtered.

When we decided to use a filter, I was pretty darned certain the ACLU and ALA would be sending a truck around to pick up my membership cards and possibly inflict on me great bodily harm. I was pretty darned certain that students would rise in revolt after having Internet search after search unreasonably blocked. I was pretty darned certain that the light of education would glow less brightly as a result of the filter's installation.

I must admit that my pragmatic side had its secret, shameful doubts about the wisdom of *not* having a filtering device installed in our district. Technology has indeed opened floodgates of information into schools by way of the Internet. And along with marvelous resources on topics of curricular and personal interest, the flotsam and sewage of the Internet had become readily available with in our walls as well. Materials and ideas that had been in the past physically inaccessible to students now could be viewed, both purposely and accidentally, at the click of a mouse button.

The potential of student access to unsavory and possibly unsafe materials on the Internet makes support of intellectual freedom extremely challenging. It is difficult to justify a resource that allows the accidental viewing of graphic sexual acts by second-graders innocently searching for information on "beavers," communication by an anorexic teen with supportive fellow anorexics, or access by seventh graders to "Build Your Own Computer Virus" Web sites. Defending unfiltered Internet access seemed quite different from defending *The Catcher in Rye.*

Yet the concept of intellectual freedom as expressed in both ALA's "Library Bill of Rights" and "Freedom to Read" statements is as relevant to information in electronic formats as it is in print:

> We trust Americans to recognize propaganda and misinformation, and to make their own decisions about what they read and believe. We do not believe they need the help of censors to assist them in this task.

I worry that while preventing access to pornographic or unsafe materials is the reason given by those who advocate restricted access to the Internet in schools, the motivation is also political: keeping impressionable minds away from particular points of view. That is censorship at its most malignant. Even though CIPA has taken the decision to use or not use Internet filters out of the hands of local decision makers, a strong commitment to intellectual freedom on the part of the school librarians, technologists, and administrators is not only possible, but even *more* important in a filtered environment.

The sky did not fall in when we installed our filter. The complaints about over-blocking from teachers and students in the past year have numbered less than a dozen. Why?

A study conducted in 2002 by the Electronic Freedom Foundation on Internet filtering devices reveals some interesting numbers:

- Schools that implement Internet blocking software with the least restrictive settings will block between 1/2 percent and 5 percent of search results based on state-mandated curriculum topics.

- Schools that implement Internet blocking software with the most restrictive settings will block up to 70 percent of search results based on state-mandated curriculum topics.

Internet filters obviously have a wide range of restrictiveness. Depending on the product, the product's settings, and the ability to override the filter to permit access to individual sites, filters can either block a high percentage of the Internet resources (specific Web sites, e-mail, chat-rooms, etc.) or a relatively small number of sites.

In our role as proponents of intellectual freedom, we need to:

- Base our choice of filters not on cost or convenience, but on features and customizability.

- Strongly advocate for the least restrictive settings of installed filters.

- Generously use the override lists in our Internet filters.

- Configure at least one machine that is completely unblocked in each library so that questionably blocked sites can be reviewed and immediately accessed by staff and students if found to be useful.

- Continue to help develop and teach the values students need to be self-regulating Internet users.

- Continue to educate and inform parents and the public about school Internet uses and issues.

- Continue to create learning environments that promote the use of the Internet for positive purposes.

I have to admit that even after crusading for filter-free Internet access for my school district and then being forced by CIPA to install a filter, the sun still rises. And in some sense, I believe our schools may even be a bit *more* ethically responsible for using a limited filtering system that keeps the little ones from accidentally accessing inappropriate or even dangerous Web sites. When chosen, configured, and monitored carefully our filter becomes a selection, rather than censorship, tool.

But I am watching it *very* closely.

So Tell Us a Little about Yourself

October 2003

Hello, DOUGLAS A JOHNSON. We have Book recommendations for you.

—Amazon.com screen

I've mentioned before how much I like science fiction's ability to predict the future, warning us of it perils and teasing us with its pleasures. Spielberg's movie *Minority Report* set me thinking about what we should be teaching our students about privacy.

In the movie, the hero is pursued through a shopping area where devices in stores biometrically read his identity and begin tailoring their sales messages directly to him. Using his previous shopping history as a source of data, the merchants are doing the ultimate "target marketing." Far fetched?

Not really. Billboards that can detect which radio station a car is receiving can change their message to fit that listener's demographic tastes. (NPR listeners get ads for environmental causes; Limbaugh listeners get ads for assault rifles?) When I log on, Amazon.com recommends titles I may be interested in based on my past purchases. Does it work? My shelf of yet-to-be-read books, many impulsively purchased from Amazon, is sagging from the weight.

"How much do you want others to know about you?" is a question we should be asking our students to ask themselves. It is a question that can only have a personal answer. But it should be an *informed* answer.

What do we need to teach kids about privacy?

Sharing information is a double-edged sword. I like it when the Web site from which I rent movies suggests a film to me that I might like. I've seen some good flicks I might otherwise have missed. But I am also aware that that knowledge of my tastes allows the site to potentially manipulate me. By telling others about ourselves, we are giving them a degree of power over us. Sharing information with marketers about one's taste in movies, books, video games, or clothing may not be very serious if students understand that this information can in turn be used to persuade them. But students should begin asking themselves who they want to know about their medical, academic, employment, or legal records.

There needs to be a balance between privacy and security. There is a good deal of debate right now regarding the government's data collection programs. By collecting vast amounts of information and mining it for patterns, the government believes it can spot and deter terrorism. Critics see it as an Orwellian plot that threatens every American's privacy. Students need to know that their privacy, especially in schools, is limited for security purposes. Backpacks, lockers, and e-mail can all be searched by school officials.

Personal information is not always collected openly. One of the scariest things about information technology is its ability to collect data about a user without the user's knowledge. Cookies, scripts within Web pages, remote monitoring programs, and hidden "spyware" can tell others what places you've visited on the Web, to whom you send e-mail, and even what programs you run—all unseen. Students need to learn to read privacy policies on Web sites and understand any school monitoring procedures in place.

American citizens have rights to data privacy and the right to see data about oneself. Student data privacy rights are usually carefully delineated by board policy and law. Libraries have their own policies regarding the protection of patron privacy. Can your students answer the following questions:

- Can your parents receive a list of the books you've checked out from the library this year?
- Can your teachers receive a list of Web sites you've visited on a particular day?
- Can your principal get a copy of the e-mails you've sent and received on your school account?
- Does your school sell lists of student names?
- Can you see all your school records, including disciplinary files?

Some kinds of data are worse to share than others. I rather like surveys. Just how often is one actually *asked* for an opinion? I will happily tell the world what I think of a restaurant, a politician, or the value of a piece of software—and sign my name. What we all need to learn to protect are our phone numbers, mailing addresses, e-mail addresses, and social security numbers.

Debate over privacy issues will rage far into the future. The policies shaped by these conversations will have a major impact on the quality of our lives. I can think of few topics of greater importance that should be part of classroom discussions, library lessons, and school policy making. Make it your responsibility to become informed.

And if you'd like to know more, just e-mail me your name and credit card number.

The Need for Community

October 2005

As I write this, Minnesotans are still in shock and mourning over the tragedy at the Red Lake School and its community. On March 21, 2005, 16-sixteen year-old student Jeff Weise brought a gun to school and killed five students and two staff members and wounded seven more before killing himself. This was after he had earlier killed his grandfather and his grandfather's companion in their home.

According to news reports, Jeff was considered an outsider in his closely knit, but impoverished community on the Red Lake reservation. He participated in online "communities"—ones that espoused violence and intolerance at nazi.org and www.abovetopsecret.com. Communities made accessible via the Internet even in his remote northern Minnesota location.

One of my first questions was how much did Jeff's access to the Internet contribute to his terrible decisions and actions? I am sure I am not the only parent, educator, or community member who wondered that had Jeff not been able to express his violent thoughts and receive support from other like-minded individuals, would he have made the choices he did?

Establishing cause and effect in incidents like these will always be speculative, and there are plenty of places at which we can point accusative fingers. Jeff's life had been horrific. He reportedly had been abused and neglected as a child. His father committed suicide and his mother lived in a nursing home after a serious car accident. Jeff was American Indian, one of our nation's most impoverished and disenfranchised minorities. And of course, the "bad seed" theory always surfaces as well. Jeff did not leave a note explaining why he took the actions he did, leaving us only sadly speculating.

One factor might be that Jeff, like all kids, looked for and did not find a sense of community "on the res." When he could not find like-minded, sympathetic, caring individuals around him physically, he looked elsewhere and found it online.

So what does this have to do with technology, libraries, and schools? We can ask how and why was Jeff "allowed" to visit and interact with others on Web hate sites? Do the dangers and risks of such groups outweigh the useful, productive resources available on the Web? Who was monitoring Jeff's Internet use? Were the adults in his life even aware such vicious places on the Internet exist? Important questions, to be sure, but to me, Jeff's Internet use ought to be considered more symptomatic than causal.

Most kids look for and find "communities" with values that are life affirming and socially responsible. Boy and Girl Scouts, 4-H clubs, church groups, and both formal and informal groups revolving around special interests such as bicycling, hunting, literature, or sports play a big role in most young people's lives as they grow up. Schools provide opportunities for socialization through athletics, music, drama, newspapers, business, or art clubs. In these groups, young people learn not just about personal interests, but also about one's fellow students and mentors and why they are worth caring about. And they are where kids often find that others care about them as well.

In our efforts to improve our schools and reduce school expenditures, the so-called extracurricular activities are often first on the chopping block. Politicians and taxpayers see music, arts, and athletics as superfluous. The "basics" are reading, writing, math, and other purely classroom pursuits. Guidance counselors, librarians, coaches, and club sponsors are nice extras only tangentially related to the real purpose of school. Sigh . . .

How many of us as librarians make a conscious effort to create "communities" for our own students, especially for those kids who do not seem to have much success with the traditional organizations? Do you have a "geek squad" in which members gain self-esteem by helping students and staff with technology problems? Do you have library volunteers who watch the circulation desk, help re-shelve materials, and create displays? As a former member of the "projector sector"— students who assisted technology-challenged teachers set-up 16mm projectors in my high school, I personally recognize how important such a seemingly small thing helped me establish a sense of belonging and camaraderie in school. And it's why I, as an educator, encourage all of us to enlist the aid of kids for whom football or band are not exactly their thing.

I am not so naïve to believe that there is a single cause of school violence or a single way to prevent it. But *St. Paul Pioneer Press* reporter David Hanners wrote, "In the online world where he felt most at home, Jeff Weise has gained more attention in death than he ever did in life." We all crave attention. What small part can we as librarians do to make sure the Jeffs in our schools get that attention in positive ways? Are we helping create communities for everyone? You never know what one thing might make a difference.

Don't Defend *That* Book

August 2007

Philosophy of Resource Selection. Public education in a democracy is committed to facilitate the educational growth and equal educational opportunity of all students. The freedom to learn, therefore, and the corresponding freedom to teach are basic to a democratic society. In order to meet these goals, School District 77 is committed to selecting educational resources which will aid student development in knowledge acquisition, critical thinking, objective evaluation and aesthetic appreciation.

—Mankato Area Public Schools Board Policy 606:
TEXTBOOKS AND INSTRUCTIONAL MATERIALS

In the spring of 2007, the discussion over the Newbery Award–winning book *The Power of Lucky* flared on LM_NET, the AASL blog, and, I am sure, in meetings, phone conversations, and e-mails throughout the country. Some librarians went nuts (pun intended) over the author using the word *scrotum* in this *children's* book.

I found it less upsetting that an anatomically correct word was used in a kiddie book and that book was given a prestigious prize, than that so many professional librarians seem to have lost the fundamental understandings of selection, reconsideration, *in loco parentis,* and intellectual freedom. Perhaps the controversy was a timely wake-up call that we all need to brush up on some of these concepts.

What troubles me is that our professional colleagues are trying to defend a single title rather than defending a fair and open process for selecting and retaining any instructional material in our schools. Quite frankly, if a school decides to remove *Lucky* or any other book from its library or classrooms, so be it. If it decides to block every Web 2.0 resource because it can't discriminate between MySpace and a professional blog, so be it. If it decides that Zeffirelli's movie *Romeo and Juliet* not be allowed because it shows a glimpse of Olivia Hussey's breasts, so be it.

So long as due process has been followed in making the decision.

While I can't imagine the circumstances under which I would do so, I sort of like knowing that as a citizen I can request that ill-chosen materials be removed from my public school. Harrumph!

As I remember from library school, this is how professionals deal with the selection of and potential censorship of instructional materials:

They assure that the district has a board adopted selection/reconsideration policy. Oh, and they've read it and they follow it.

They select all materials based on the stated selection criteria in the policy. Ours here in Mankato include:

- Considering the characteristics and philosophy of the school and community when selecting resources.

- Providing resources that will enrich and support the curriculum, taking into consideration the varied interests, abilities, and maturity levels of the individuals served.

- Providing resources relative to controversial issues so that individuals may develop informed opinions and practice critical reading and thinking.

- Providing resources representative of the many religious, ethnic, and cultural groups and their contributions to our American heritage.

- Placing principle above personal opinion and reason above prejudice in the selection of resources of the highest quality in order to assure a comprehensive collection appropriate for the users.

They select only materials based on authoritative and reliable review sources.

If they are asked to remove an item selected from the instructional program, they do not defend the material, but insist that the board adopted reconsideration policy and procedures be followed. This policy should require that a standing reconsideration committee be appointed at the beginning of each school year. When requested by the committee, they provide the rationale and resources used for selection of the item under reconsideration.

Once a resource is selected, they do not restrict its use by any student. Professionals cannot act in the place of parents (*in loco parentis*) to restrict access to materials to individuals. (You think when serving a thousand kids, I can remember the restrictions individual parents want me to put on their kids?)

It's just that easy! Know your selection policy, select from authoritative reviews, insist on due process if a book is challenged, and make children responsible for their own choices.

It's not hard, but it *does* take genuine courage. And it is not only why we need professionals in all our school libraries, but professionals who act professionally.

At some point in time, schools will need to wake up and realize that the principles of selection and reconsideration also need to apply to online resources, including the Web sites. Does your district have a written policy that upholds the concepts of intellectual freedom in regard to the Internet? Who decides what is blocked and how are those decisions made?

I hope there aren't other basic principles I've forgotten. Library school was, after all, many, many, many years ago.

A Father-Son Chat

November 2007

My son Brady, like many Net Genners, is not just a consumer of creative products but a producer as well. When I learned he was about to have one of his drawings published by a national journal, I gave him this fatherly advice. It might be something you wish to share with your creative students as well.

Dear Son,

I understand that a national publication has asked to publish your work. I have always been proud of your wit, skill, and creativity, and it is wonderful to see it recognized by the editors of a high quality magazine.

But it is time to have a little father-son talk about "reproductive" rights. I know how heady that feeling can be when you realize someone wants you, thinks you are wonderful. But son, please don't let this new relationship blind you to some realities of life. You may not want to hear this, but I say it only to protect you.

Look carefully at the language of the copyright agreement the Publisher wants you to sign:

> Author hereby grants to Publisher all right, title, interest in and to the Work, including copyright in all means of expression by any method now known or hereafter developed, including electronic format . . .

Are you really willing to give up *all* rights to your baby—forever? You will never be able to use it again without asking permission of this first publisher. The publisher can use and reuse and sell your creative work again and again if it so chooses in any format, to any other publisher, no matter how low and degraded. Is this really what you want?

I am old man. Maybe not as old as you think but I have been around the track a few times. Let me give you a suggestion. Send in your own publication agreement. Word it something like this:

> The Author hereby grants the Publisher the exclusive right to the first publication of the Work in the _____ (date or volume) edition of _____ (title of publication) in print format only. This exclusive right extends for 90 days after publication, after which the Author may republish the Work in any format or resell to any publisher. A separate permission must be granted for any use of the Work in any other issue of the publication, in any other publication, or in any other format. The Publisher may not resell the Work or grant permission to any other entity to use the Work without the Author's written consent. The Author retains exclusive copyright ownership of the Work.

What is the worst that can happen? The publisher will say "no" and negotiations will continue.

Your generation of producers often views the use of others' creative work as raw material for their own expressions. The term "mashup" and "remix" are commonly used to describe a montage of digital works—especially music and video—that have been combined and edited to create a unique creative product. The use of others' work is regarded not as theft or plagiarism, but homage to the originator, and sites like *YouTube* make sharing such creations simple and inexpensive.

So another avenue you, my boy, may wish to explore is granting a CopyLeft-type permission so others can use your work. The recognition that one's own work can and should be used by others in their own creative processes has given rise to a new means of intellectual property control called Creative Commons. The movement, started by Stanford Law School professor and author Lawrence Lessig in 2001, is a backlash against what many see as overly restrictive copyright laws that keep intellectual property out of the public domain for an unreasonably long period of time. But by using a Creative Commons license, the intellectual property creator (that's you) openly gives others varying degrees of rights to use the property in the belief the work can be used, changed, and improved upon by others.

Your creative work is what will sustain you financially and emotionally throughout your career. Learn to treat it well, guard it carefully, and value it highly. Your father wants to make sure you earn enough money from your imagination and skills to place him in a nursing home of high quality as he enters his dotage.

Publishers are seductive, but they usually have their own best interests at heart, not yours.

Love,

Dad

From Cop to Counselor on Copyright

October 2008

Most of us shudder when asked a question about the fair use of copy-righted materials. "Uh, the poster over the copier says I can only use a poem of less than 250 words in my project and this poem is 251 words. Am I breaking the law?" Been to law school recently enough to know how to answer that question?

Actually law school may not help you much. Fair use guidelines are, well, guidelines, subject to interpretation. Temple University professors Hobbs, Jaszi, and Aufderheide (2008) wisely write: "Applying fair use reasoning is about reaching a level of comfort, not memorizing a specific set of rules." There are no definitive answers to the question "Is this fair use?"

So, how do we help our teachers and students establish an informed, personal "level of comfort"?

Few of us are comfortable at either extreme of copyright enforcement—playing the copyright bully *or* completely ignoring situations of ques-tionable copyrighted materials use. Complicating the issue is that each of us is likely to arrive at his/her own personal level of fair use comfort, judgment of seriousness of possible use, and perspective of the morality of intellectual property use both personally and professionally.

I propose we librarians re-brand ourselves, "copyright counselors," and do what good counselors have always done—help others reach good decisions about their actions rather than serve in a judgmental role.

Allow me to advance some practical steps to teach and enforce copyright compliance and other issues of intellectual property use. Raise your right hand, stand on one foot, and repeat after me:

I will acknowledge that the enforcement of all laws and policies is an administrative responsibility, not mine. Quite honestly, if a building principal chooses not to learn about copyright, about how materials are being used in her building, or about whether district policies are being broken, it is not the librarian's job to make her. She's the one getting paid the big bucks. Let her earn them.

I will rat out my fellow teachers only under a very narrow set of circumstances. There are copyright infringements so egregious that you should bring them to your boss's attention. But, they need to be something that carries a genuine risk of generating a lawsuit. Put your concerns in writing, include examples of this type of use causing harm to other schools, send it only once, and keep a CYA copy. (E-mail me if you want to know what CYA means.)

I need not commit any acts I deem illegal. If a teacher asks you to make a copy of something and you feel it does not fit under *your* personal view of fair use guidelines, you will politely say "no" and explain why. And probably teach him how make the copy himself.

In in-services and communications, I will emphasize what *can,* not what *can't,* be done with intellectual property. You will stress "fair use," give open source options to software, and alert your staff to royalty free, public domain, and Creative Commons sources. Change your role from enforcer to enabler. If someone asks you specifically whether a use is legal or illegal, you will respond: "It depends on your personal philosophy. If you can justify that the use meets fair use guidelines, is transformational, and sets a good example for your students, go for it!"

I will make sure any signs about fair use will be accompanied by a caveat. If you have a sign hanging over the photocopier with a long list of fair use guidelines make a sign of your own that reads, "This chart states only 'safe harbor' guidelines and is not an authoritative legal statement. More flexible uses and amounts may apply under certain circumstances." Paste it to the other sign.

I will teach copyright to students from the viewpoint of the creator.
You will ask students to assign a Creative Commons designation to each
piece of original work they produce—especially those items they will be
sharing online or publishing. By thinking about how one wants his/her
own work treated, one is forced to consider the rights and wishes of
other IP creators as well. Counsel teachers to use a CC designation on
their work as well.

My long-standing philosophy is that education is about teaching others
to think rather than *to believe.* It's our job as librarians to help both
students and teachers arrive at personal comfort levels when using
protected creative works.

Reflection

> Always do right. This will gratify some people and astonish the rest.
>
> —Mark Twain

Let me start right out with an admission: I am no more or less ethical than
most people. And given that the "righteous crusader" exposed for some
slimy breach of morality has become so common it is now a stereotype,
one would need to be a genuine idiot to claim anything else. I am just
waiting for the dirt to be revealed about Mother Teresa's hidden bank
accounts. Don't turn to me as a good example of anything. I can't take
the pressure.

And as I start my workshops on ethical issues, I truthfully state that I
don't have all the answers. I can only leave those in attendance "confused at a higher level."

I have also found in all my years as a teacher that I have been unable to
instill a "value" in anyone else—students, teachers, friends, or my own
children. And least of all, my wife. Not that her values (other than her
taste in men) aren't just fine as they are. But what I can do is present
good information to others when a situation involving ethics arises and
foster conversations that help others come to hopefully better conclusions.
The line is a fine one between *rationale* and *rationalization.* I like to
think rationales have thoughtful data behind them.

The flip side of developing ethics is helping people live safely. For me,
ethics is doing the right thing; safety is knowing how to recognize and
protect oneself from the unethical actions of others.

Schools need to be places that let students make "safe" mistakes with
technology, allowing them to develop their powers of judgment. Coach

John Wooden famously said, "If you're not making mistakes, then you're not doing anything." A big part of learning is about making errors and figuring out how not to repeat them. A middle school student who shares her password with a friend who then destroys files is a recoverable mistake—one that she will remember before sharing her bankcard PIN number as an adult.

Such environments can be scary places for us adults who have custodial responsibilities for children and young adults. It's why, in our fear, we have installed Internet filters and denied access to social networking sites in schools along with banning books. But as Carol Simpson lectures:

> Trying to teach students to use the Internet through a filtered computer is like teaching a child to cross the street in the basement. They'll be run down the first time they try to cross a real street because they've had no guided experience.

Intellectual freedom, privacy rights, and intellectual property concerns are all areas with which our professional library training should have extensively dealt. But the reality is that ethical issues have become a moving target as technologies create huge opportunities for information use and misuse.

But maintaining our core values—understanding the concepts of intellectual freedom; being aware that most moral judgments center around privacy, property, and appropriate use; and believing that individuals should act out of awareness, not ignorance—will help all of us make choices that allow us to sleep well at night.

On reflection, values clarifier may be our most important role as librarian. If we don't do it, who in our schools will?

Afterword: Why I Write for Publication (and You Should Too)

Earlier version published on AASL's KQWeb, *May 2001*

I write professionally for the big bucks, huge prestige, and pure adulation of millions of fans. While the limos, champagne on first class flights, and attractive strangers constantly opening their bank accounts and boudoirs to me can get tiresome, having my own line of fashion apparel saves me from having to shop for clothes.

Oh wait, that's some other kind of writer. I write for professional publications, like library journals. Sorry, I got lost in fantasy for a moment. . .

Let's see, so why do I write? There are a number of pretty good reasons I why write (and why you, dear reader, should consider doing so as well):

1. *I have to write anyway.* Much of what I write about comes from dealing with challenges on my day job as library and technology director for Mankato Public Schools. As a part of making an effective library program work, tools need to be developed, policies written, programs planned, and philosophies clarified. Things seem to run better in my district when they are down in black and white. Prob-

lems, new projects, and good questions from students, staff, and the public all require that I write about them, even if it is only to help me clarify my own thinking. And I figure that if I am struggling with an issue, others may be as well.

2. *Writing keeps me current.* There is no incentive like knowing others will be reading what one has written to force one to stay current on technologies and trends in education. I like reading futurists, and it's a real challenge to try to figure out the implications of their predictions for my school and profession. While I was never much for doing "research" in high school or college, using information to find solutions to problems is actually interesting. I still detest having to write things like the Works Cited pages that follow, however.

3. *Writing helps me keep my day job (I hope).* I mess up on my job a lot. Anyone who really tries out new methods of teaching and working should be expected to fail on a regular basis. If you don't, you are probably not reaching far enough. So every now and then it is nice to be able to slip an article or column to the superintendent, board member, or even a member of my own staff. Perhaps their thinking goes, "Gee, others think this guy has some credibility. Maybe he isn't as crazy as *I* think he is."

4. *Publishing returns the favor to others from whom I have borrowed.* I have learned so much from the people I consider to be the *real* experts in libraries and technology. A partial list includes Loertscher, Eisenberg, Simpson, Berger, Barron, Valenza, Haycock, Donham, Jukes, McKenzie, and a whole raft of bloggers who represent the best minds of the next generation of thinkers. And it isn't just the big dogs who help me: I steal my *best* ideas from practicing librarians and technologists who speak at conferences, write for journals, and contribute to LM_NET. I am a great believer in the "stone soup" mentality. When everyone contributes to the pot, the soup is richer for it.

5. *Knowing I've helped someone.* It's the rare conference or week of e-mails when I don't get a thank-you from a librarian or technologist who tells me they have been able to some how use what I've written. Whether it is a tool that they've found effective, the description of a plan that they've gotten to work in their district, or a column that persuaded a local decision maker, wonderful people come forward to say thank you. It makes all the sunny mornings I spend writing instead of playing worth it. Thanks again back to you.

6. *I'm on a mission from God.* Heavens knows that nobody goes into education (or writes for it) to make money. As educators, our satisfaction comes from actually believing we are doing something that

will make the world a more humane place in which to live. The ultimate goal of professional writing is to improve professional practice that in turn improves the lives of kids and in turn improves the world. Minnesota writer Fredrick Manfred in his poem "The Old Black Silence" says it far better than I ever could:

. . .Open up and let go.
Even if it's only blowing. But blast.
And I say this loving my God.
Because we are all he has at last.
So what about it, boy?
Is your work going well?
Are you still lighting lamps
Against darkness and hell?

7. *Finally, I just love making lists.* I not only encourage but expect all members of the library profession to write for publication. While it may never improve your bank account, you'll get jewels in your crown for lighting those lamps against darkness and hell.

And please, toss in a little humor and poetry when you do.

Works Cited

American Association of School Librarians. "Standards for the 21st-Century Learner," American Library Association, 2007.

Associated Press. "Who Shall We Kill Tonight?" *Wired,* May 8, 2006. http://www. wired.com/news/culture/0,70839-0.html?tw=rss.index (accessed 9/14/2009).

Baron, Naomi. "Killing the Written Word by Snippets." *Los Angeles Times,* November 28, 2005, B11. http://articles.latimes.com/2005/nov/28/opinion/oe-baron28.

Bridges, William. *Surviving Corporate Transition: Rational Management in a World of Mergers, Layoffs, Start-ups, Takeovers, Divestitures, Deregulation, and New Technologies.* New York: Doubleday, 1991.

Buckingham, Betty Jo, and Barbara Safford. *Weeding the Library Media Collections.* Des Moines: State of Iowa Department of Education, 1994.

Casner-Lotto, Jill. *Are They Really Ready to Work?: Employers' Perspectives on the Basic Knowledge and Applied Skills of New Entrants to the 21st Century U.S. Workforce.* Tucson, AZ: Partnership for 21st Century Skills, 2006.

Consumers Union. "Guidelines for Evaluating SOCAP & IOCU Materials." 1998. www.consumersunion.org/other/captivekids/guidelines.htm

Conway, Ruth. National Association of Independent Schools Reporter, Spring 1994.

Covey, Stephen. *The 7 Habits of Highly Effective People: Restoring the Character Ethic.* New York: Fireside, 1990.

Csikszentmihalyi, Mihaly. *Flow: The Psychology of Optimal Experience.* New York: Harper, 1990.

Dillard, Annie. *The Writing Life.* New York: Harper Perennial, 1990.

Ehrenreich, Barbara. *Nickel and Dimed: On (Not) Getting By in America.* New York: Metropolitan, 2001.

Foster, Andrea. "Students Lack 'Information Literacy,' Testing Service's Study Finds." *Chronicle of Higher Education,* October 27, 2006. http://chronicle.com/article/Students-Fall-Short-on-Inf/27038/.

Hanner, David. *Weise's words, images keep Web buzzing.* Pioneer Press, April 10, 2005.

Hobbs, Renee, Peter Jaszi, and Patricia Aufderheide. *Ten Common Misunderstandings about Fair Use.* Philadelphia: Temple University Media Education Lab, 2008.

International Society for Technology in Education. "ISTE National Educational Technology Standards (NETS•S) and Performance Indicators for Students," 2007.

Jupiter Research."Online consumers spend as much time online as in front of the TV" JupiterReports, January 2006. http://www.jupitermedia.com/corporate/releases/06.01.30-newjupresearch.html.

Kohn, Alfie. *Punished by Rewards: The Trouble With Gold Stars, Incentive Plans, A's, Praise, and Other Bribes.* Boston: Houghton Mifflin, 1993.

Kozol, Jonathan. *Savage Inequalities: Children in America's Schools.* New York: Harper, 1991.

KRC Research. *A report of findings from six focus groups with K–12 parents, teachers, principals, as well as middle and high school students.* Chicago: ALA, 2003.

Lee, Harper. To Kill a Mockingbird. New York: Harper, 1960.

Lenhart, Amanda, and Mary Madden. *Teen Content Creators and Consumers.* Washington, DC: Pew Internet & American Life Project, 2005.

Lewis, David W. "Eight Truths for Middle Managers in Lean Times." *Library Journal*, September 1, 1991.

Manrred, Frederick. *Winter count: the poems of Frederick Manfred.* University of California: Thorp Springs Press, 1977

Masie, Elliott. "Low Cost Home Based Wireless Modem; Learners Are One Click Away From Leaving; Changes in IT Training Are Coming!" *Elliott Masie's Learning Trends.* August 17, 1998. http://trends.masie.com/archives/month/august-1998.

Mick, Haley. "Socially Awkward? Hit the Books." (*Toronto*) *Globe and Mail.* July 10, 2008. http://www.theglobeandmail.com/servlet/story/RTGAM.20080710. wlreading10/BNStory/lifeMain/home.

Moran, Robert. *Never Confuse a Memo with Reality: And Other Business Lesson Too Simple Not to Know.* New York: Harper, 1994.

Murnane, Richard. *Teaching the New Basic Skills: Principles for Educating Children to Thrive in a Changing Economy.* New York: Free Press, 1997.

National Endowment of the Arts. "Reading At Risk: A Survey of Literary Reading in America," June 2004. http://www.nea.gov/pub/ReadingAtRisk.pdf (accessed 9/14/2009).

Nie and Hillygus. "Where does Internet time come from? A Reconnaissance." IT&SOCIETY, Fall 2002. http://www.stanford.edu/group/siqss/itandsociety/v01i02/v01i02a01.pdf (accessed 9/14/2009).

Norman, Donald. *Things That Make Us Smart: Defending Human Attributes in the Age of the Machine.* Reading, MA: Addison-Wesley, 1994.

Oblinger, Diane and James Oblinger. *Educating the Net Generation.* EDCAUSE, 2005. http://net.educause.edu/ir/library/pdf/pub7101.pdf.

Payne, Ruby. *A Framework for Understanding Poverty.* Highlands, TX: aha! Process, 2003.

Pink, Daniel. *A Whole New Mind: Why Right-Brainers Will Rule the Future.* New York: Riverhead Books, 2006.

Postman, Neil, and Charles Weingartner. *Teaching as a Subversive Activity.* New York: Dell Publishing, 1969.

Ravitch, Diane. *The Language Police: How Pressure Groups Restrict What Students Learn.* New York: Knopf, 2003.

Severance, Darlene. "Supervising Library Paraprofessionals." *Tallahassee Freenet.* http://www.tfn.net/Liberty_Library/para.html.

Simpson, Carol. Internet filtering—the debate continues. *Technology & Learning,* April, 2000.

Surowiecki, James. *The Wisdom of Crowds.* New York: Doubleday, 2004.

Tapscott, Don. *Growing Up Digital: the Rise of the Net Generation.* New York: McGraw Hill, 1999.

Valenza, Joyce. "Springfield Township High School Library Annual Report—June 2006." Springfield Township High School. http://www.sdst.org/shs/library/documents/annualreport06.pdf

About the Author and Illustrator

Doug Johnson has been the Director of Media and Technology for the Mankato (MN) Public Schools since 1991, and has served as an adjunct faculty member of Minnesota State University since 1990. His teaching experience has included work in grades K–12 both here and in Saudi Arabia. He is the author of four other books: *The Indispensable Librarian, The Indispensable Teacher's Guide to Computer Skills, Teaching Right from Wrong in the Digital Age,* and *Machines are the Easy Part; People are the Hard Part.* His regular columns appear in *Library Media Connection* and on the *Education World* Web site. Doug's Blue Skunk Blog averages over 50,000 visits a month, and his articles have appeared in over 40 books and periodicals. Doug has conducted workshops and given presentations for over 130 organizations throughout the United States as well as in Malaysia, Kenya, Thailand, Germany, Qatar, Canada, Chile, Peru, the United Arab Emirates, and Australia and has held a variety of leadership positions in state and national organizations, including International Society for Technology in Education (ISTE) and American Association of School Librarians (AASL).

Brady Johnson is a Film and Video Arts School graduate who has recently been living and working in Wellington, New Zealand. His illustrations can be found on the Blue Skunk blog, in the book *Machines Are the Easy Part; People are the Hard Part* and in issues of AASL's *Knowledge Quest* journal. He is currently pursuing the completion of various (and maybe a bit twisted) illustrations and comic projects of his own. He can be contacted at: brady13yoshi@yahoo.com.